CW01573966

Armchair Hik

In the Western C

MIKE LUNDY

Armchair Hiking
in the Western Cape

with illustrations by Tony Grogan

Human & Rousseau
Cape Town   Pretoria   Johannesburg

Copyright © 1999 by Mike Lundy
First published in 1999 by
Human & Rousseau (Pty) Ltd,
Design Centre, 179 Loop Street, Cape Town
Cover design and typography by Anna-Marie Petzer
Typeset in 11.5 on 13 pt Times New Roman by ALINEA STUDIO, Cape Town
Printed and bound by National Book Printers,
Drukkery Street, Goodwood, Western Cape

ISBN 0 7981 3938 2

Acknowledgements

Evelyn John Holtzhausen, erstwhile night editor of the *Cape Times* – you got me into this in the first place. You persuaded me to become a journalist in my spare time, but little did I know you were injecting printing ink into my veins. Highly addictive and very exciting. I have no regrets.

To my various editors over a four-year period at the *Cape Times Top of the Times* weekend magazine and the *Sunday Times Cape Metro*. Thank you, Tony Jackman, Adele Sulcas, Donald Paul and Ray Joseph for not "hacking" my work – even when I was sometimes deliberately contentious.

Cape Union Mart has always given me great support in the sale of my books and hiking gear. They willingly volunteered to sponsor the illustrations in this book, which I sincerely appreciate.

Tony Grogan for his wonderful talent of being able to turn the written word into a descriptive illustration in literally seconds. I have often wished I could do that, along with playing the piano and speaking French. I am totally incapable of all three.

My editor, Riëtte Botma, for her quiet efficiency and always delivering the goods on time.

Contents

WESTERN CAPE MIDDLE DISTANCE

Introduction

This is a book to read whilst you are passing time on the loo. Or in your favourite armchair . . . or just prior to nodding off in bed with your spectacles hanging precariously from one ear.

It is a book which I hope will take your mind to high places, where you will discover many wondrous things about nature along with fascinating snippets of local history.

Did you know, for example, that you would pick up a higher level of radiation by taking a two-hour flight to Johannesburg, than if you were to sit naked for one year on the perimeter fence of Koeberg Nuclear Power Station? Not that you would really wish to expose yourself to the vagaries of a Cape winter, but that is a startling fact. What if I were to tell you that *gewone bokdrol* is a tree and cuckoo spit is insect pooh? And do you know that Cape Point is the windiest spot on the African continent? Or that the blue whale is the largest creature that has ever lived on this planet, weighing in at the size of thirty elephants?

No? Well, then read on.

But heaven forbid you should actually want to *walk* any of these hikes. That seems much too much like hard work. No. Much better you stay put, read a bit, learn a bit and maybe laugh a bit. Then think about it again. Who knows, you might actually want to go and discover these amazing things for yourself. They're really just on your doorstep – if you know where to look. It's a *fascinating* world out there. Enjoy it!

MIKE LUNDY
August 1999

CAPE PENINSULA

The Noon Gun

Freezing the balls
off a brass monkey

It really has been cold enough lately to freeze the balls off a brass monkey. Which reminds me of a rather delightful little walk to the Noon Gun. But what on earth have these things got to do with each other? You may well ask. Perhaps a lot more than my prissy old Aunt Agatha might ever dare to imagine.

In the old days, fighting ships carried on deck, next to each gun, a brass triangle known as a monkey. It was merely three strips of brass joined together, and its purpose was to contain the pyramid of cannonballs placed within it. In freezing conditions, the brass contracted more than the iron and the whole shooting match came tumbling down.

So you see, Aunt Agatha – it's all to do with different coeffiecients of expansion and contraction, and nothing whatsoever to do with what you were thinking . . .

In fact, even Aunt Agatha could do this downhill doddle. It starts from the parking area at the very end of Signal Hill Road (rather indelicately, from the public toilets there). Cross over the tar road to get onto a Jeep track and follow it for twenty minutes and a little more than a kilometre to the fascinating Lion Battery, from which Cape Town's world-famous Noon Gun is fired.

Along the way, you will be treated to aerial views of Green Point Common, followed by the Waterfront, the Foreshore, harbour and, finally, Schotschekloof.

Cape Town is special in many ways – not least of all for its Noon Gun. The only other cities in the world that fire a noon gun are Hong Kong and Rome, but both of these are fairly recent innovations. The tradition has been around in the Mother City since 1806 – nearly 200 years.

Originally, it was fired from the Imhoff Battery at the castle but, when the city began to expand, it was moved to Signal Hill in 1902.

The gun is fired electronically by landline from the observatory, in the suburb of Observatory, at precisely noon. The atomic clock there has an accuracy close to one-millionth of a second – which is a little over the top, to say the least.

Such incredible precision is no longer needed for our purposes.

But in the not-so-far-off days when ships depended heavily on the accuracy of their chronometers for navigation, Cape Town's noon gun had the very practical purpose of allowing ships in the bay to reset their time pieces accurately.

However, as the sound would take six or seven seconds to reach them out at anchor (representing a sizable error in navigational terms), the gunpowder is formulated to give off a large puff of smoke, so that noon is when you *see* it, not when you hear it. One indignant old gentleman, living in Milnerton, once phoned the Lion Battery to tell them that they were consistently eleven seconds late in firing the Noon Gun. He cited the BBC pips as his evidence. It must have been somewhat deflating to be told that the sound takes consistently eleven seconds to reach Milnerton.

The Noon Gun is fired every day except for Sundays and public holidays, and recently celebrated its 60 000th firing. The battery is open to the public from eleven to one pm on firing days.

Oh, sorry, Aunt Agatha, I forgot to tell you. If you haven't arranged transport to pick you up, you're going to have to walk all the way back up the hill again.

Hmm . . . Bang goes that idea.

Cape Times, August 8, 1997

A world of trees in Tokai

Planted more than a century ago

Rex and Fido would blow their minds here. If not their bladders. Just imagine a canine heaven where you can lift you leg against the most exotic and interesting tree trunks to be found in any forest in the world. This puts lampposts in a seriously down-market position.

If you think an oak is just an oak, then think again. Take a look at the Tokai Arboretum. This arboreal United Nations is home to Turkish oaks, Algerian oaks, Australian silky oaks, cork oaks and willow oaks.

South African okes are conspicious by their absence, for this place is home to just about any foreign tree you care to mention.

You want pines? Try the Apache pines or the Canary Island pines for size. No, on second thoughts, for size you've got to try Californian redwoods. Dogs *dream* about Californian redwoods.

Then there's jarrah from Australia, different cypresses from Arizona, Mexico and the Himalayas. And much, much more.

This fascinating collection of trees are individually labelled, telling you from which corner of the globe they come. The circular walk is along a clearly marked, well-defined path, without any great effort required. It's a walk in the park. But definitely not your average common or garden park.

To get to the Tokai Arboretum, aim for the well-known Tokai Manor House, situated between the upmarket Steenberg Estate and Golf Course and the slopes of Constantiaberg.

The arboretum is some 300 metres behind and to the left of the Manor House, itself a fine example of Cape Dutch architecture.

Before starting the walk, pop in to the information centre, just inside the entrance. There are numerous interesting displays on the fauna, flora, birds, geology and even the mushrooms of the area.

The circular path begins about forty paces up the gravel track from the entrance. You will be given a self-guided tour of the forest if you merely follow the numbered poles back to the information centre. The circuit will take a leisurely 25 minutes.

The redwoods (*Sequoia sp.*) were planted in 1903 and are a bit higher

up than the circular walk will take you. But if you wish to marvel at them, this is a separate mission. Ask the gate attendant for details.

"Arboretum" means tree garden and that's just what it is, spread over quite a large chunk of land. The Tokai Arboretum was established in 1885, which means that many of its residents are well over a hundred years old.

It was started by Joseph Lister as a research project to establish which exotic trees could be exploited in the Cape Colony. What we now have in forestry plantations throughout South Africa is as a direct result of his research.

Nursery Ravine, above Kirstenbosch, owes its name to him, for he established a similar arboretum at the top of the ravine, which became known as the Lister Nursery.

Although the original purpose of the Tokai Arboretum has been fulfilled, it has been decided to keep it going for its educational and historical value. Thinking of which, that costs money, so feed the donations box at the entrance generously.

Oh, sorry, I forgot to tell you. No dogs allowed. It could be just *too* much strain for them.

Cape Times, August 15, 1997

Cape of Good Hope to Cape Point

Windiest place in Africa

The Land God Made in Anger has been said to describe Namibia, but He must have been in a pretty grotty mood when He made Cape Point

According to the meteorologists, this is the most wind-exposed place on the African continent. The wind blows here at an *average* speed of 35 km/h throughout the entire year. That's windy. But in spite of the ruffled hair and runny noses, do not avoid this place. You would be missing something very different.

Many people seem to think that Cape Point and the Cape of Good Hope are the same thing. Well, a miss is as good as a mile. And that's about the size of it. This beautiful scenic walk is just that – a mile – or 1,6 km. The bonus at the end of it is a superbly positioned restaurant with a view to die for. Which is probably the fate you will wish on the hordes of tourists you have to wade your way through when you get there. Just close your eyes and think of pounds and dollars and yen and marks.

The first ten minutes of this walk will take your breath away, both literally and figuratively. Get to the start by following the road signs to Cape of Good Hope (not Cape Point), where a signboard offers you the profoundly useless information that you are now at the "South-Western-most point of the African Continent".

Wow! . . . So what?

Southernmost or Westernmost I can understand might have some significance for those who care. But this is rather like being half pregnant. I've actually seen people standing proudly in front of this notice and having their photographs taken, as if it were at the very edge of the world. Avoid being seen too close to it.

Of equal insignificance is the useless fact that I live in the highest West-North-West facing house in Hout Bay.

The steep log steps at the start will lead you, after ten minutes, to a viewpoint which you will not forget easily. You will be presented with an incredible drop and a spectacular view of Cape Point, normally only seen by passing ships.

Once up the initial steep climb, the rest is a gentle gradient, a lot of it on boardwalks to protect the veg-

etation. In all, it will take you 45 minutes. A bit outside the qualifying time for a four-minute mile – but who cares? This is for pleasure. Should you find yourself without a kindly uncle or understanding spouse to pick you up at the end, the return route is only 35 minutes. Same path but downhill.

Most tourists using the brand new funicular railway to reach the lighthouse from the parking area of Cape Point assume that this is *the* lighthouse. But Cape Point has not one, but two lighthouses. The "tourist" lighthouse hasn't shone its guiding light for a long time. It was a bureaucratic bungle. Erected in 1857, it was soon found to be pretty useless. At a height of 211 me-

tres above sea level, it was often muffled by cloud but very visible in clear weather – precisely when it wasn't needed. One can't help being reminded of a lighthouse in the desert. Brilliant but useless.

When the *Lusitania* was wrecked in foggy weather on the rocks below in 1911, the message became clear, if not the lighthouse. It was decided to correct the mistake and build another one lower down. This one is only 71 metres above sea level, but visible in most kinds of weather.

Which just goes to show. A ship on the rocks is worth two on the cliff. Or something like that.

Cape Times, August 22, 1997

The Liesbeek trail

A history
runs through it

The Liesbeek River, birthplace of the South African economy, runs through the history of the Cape like a silver thread. It is possible to amble alongside, or very close to, the river, all the way from Kirstenbosch to Observatory. But near each end it is necessary to walk along tar roads. That's about as infra dig as picking your nose in parliament (it happened on TV the other day).

So, to remain a purist and avoid being run over by a No. 9 bus, stick to the bit in the middle which has a constructed footpath along the banks of the river. This will also ensure that you end, conveniently, at a most pleasant venue in a tranquil setting where you can have a light meal and a beer or three. Then catch the train back to your car from Newlands station, remembering to get off two stops up the line at Rosebank station. The walk is three kilometres long and should take about 45 minutes. A bonus for handicapped people is that the route is wheelchair friendly.

Lies means reeds and *beek* is the Dutch word for a stream, so the "Liesbeek River" is one of those linguistic repetitions. Clearly, the National Place Names Commission was asleep at the time. Anyway, now that it's mostly been formed into a canal, reeds can only be seen in the lower reaches.

The Friends of the Liesbeek (they got it right) is a society keen to introduce you to the river's flowers, birds and trees – and the story of our rainbow nation, for its birth cries were first heard on the banks of this river. They do regular guided hikes along the upper section from Kirstenbosch to the Josephine Mill, next to Newlands rugby ground. To make a booking phone them on (021) 686-4939.

The section described here is not guided. Either way, you'll still finish at Josephine Mill where refreshments can be had in tranquil surroundings next to the river.

For this section start at the corner of Alma Road and Liesbeek Parkway near Rosebank station, taking the second footbridge to the right over the river and under the railway line. Then, follow the railway line for 150 metres before rejoining the river. The rest is easy to follow.

Soon you will pass close to Rondebosch Fountain. On or near this spot stood a clump of thorn trees which gave Rondebosch its original name – *'t Ronde Doornbosjen*. The fountain, one of Cape Town's two remaining street horse troughs, was donated by George Pigot Moodie in 1891. This colourful character, a Transvaal mining pioneer, lived for part of each year in what is now Genadendal – Madiba's *plekkie* next to Groote Schuur. He ran an electric cable from what was then called Westbrook to light the fountain at night. It thus became the first suburban electric streetlight in the country.

You will know when your walk is near its end from the strong smell of hops. No less than seven breweries used to operate along the banks of the Liesbeek. Long-forgotten breweries like Mariendahl, Canon, Cloetes and Letterstedt were taken over by Swedish immigrant Anders Ohlsson. Born out of this takeover is the modern-day SA Breweries. (Now the fourth largest brewer in the world, with newly acquired international interests.)

Josephine Mill signals the end of the walk and an opportunity for refreshment. It is Cape Town's only surviving and operational water mill and was built in 1840 by another Swedish immigrant – Jakob Letterstedt. He named it after Crown Princess Josephine of his native Sweden. Part of his prosperous and diversified activities included milling and brewing. Not that you will need reminding of the beer at the end of this walk.

Cape Times, August 29, 1997

Kalk Bay hillside

Time to
smell the flowers

Imagine this retired rugger-bugger, somewhat portly, somewhat past his prime – 189 cm and 93 kg – throwing himself to the ground on the mountainside above St James, *to smell a flower*.

That's right, a flower. And the faraway look in his eyes tells you he's really freaked out by this flower.

"What kind of *moffie* is this?" I hear you say.

Well, it's me. *Moi*. Himself. (Well, not *terribly* portly and only *just* over the hill.)

But the flower – that's really something. It's called *Erica urnaviridis*, and it grows on this mountain between Muizenberg and Kalk Bay and *nowhere else in the world*. Not even just around the corner in Constantia, where they have most things.

What's more, it's growing there right now, and its delicate beauty, magnified by its rarity, is something to behold. The name means "erica (or heath) shaped like a green urn".

Spring has sprung, so go and see it on a gentle mountain climb, with superb views over False Bay, a vista from Hangklip to Simon's Town and Kalk Bay harbour nestling peacefully below. And you'll be surprised at the height to which you climb, with very little effort.

Start on the bend in the road just south of a house labeled No. 110 Boyes Drive, almost opposite St James railway station. Leave another car (or walk back) on Boyes Drive, 1,5 km further south, opposite the Kalk Bay Harbour entrance.

The path climbs from the start ever so gently in the direction of Simon's Town, while running parallel to Boyes Drive. You might almost get the impression that Boyes Drive is dropping away below you, rather than you rising above it. Listen for the clickety-clack of a passing train and take in the picturesque fishing harbour below.

Within half an hour you will suddenly come to the end of a gravel road, marked rather rudely by a rubbish bin. The reason for its presence is some rather pleasant picnic spots in this rocky area known as Ou Kraal.

Turn left at this T-junction and a few metres further on, take the fork downhill to a pleasant little water-

ing hole called Weary Willy's, under some indigenous trees. You might like to linger here for a while and take in the tranquillity.

Cross over the stream and turn left to follow it on its gurgling way down the mountainside to your waiting car.

On the way, keep your eyes peeled for the precious little green urns. I can hear my friend Paul saying, "It's only a bloody *flower*!"

Well I don't like ballet and Beethoven, so there!

Cape Times, September 5, 1997

The Woodcutter's Trail

Hampton Court Maze, eat your heart out

Circles in the Forest was a well-known book and play a few years back – but that's what you're likely to make if you decide to tackle the Woodcutter's Trail in Newlands Forest.

The forest is a maze of unmarked and unmapped paths and the trail is poorly signposted. Your chances, therefore, of losing your way are pretty good. But heavens, don't let that put you off.

Wherever you finish up will be a pleasure. And there's always the knowledge that your car and the freeway are at the bottom of the slope, so you can never get seriously lost.

I have this vision of an aging Japanese soldier staggering out of the undergrowth and offering to surrender . . . But that's just my fertile imagination getting silly.

The route is almost entirely in shade and a large part of it is along the banks of the Newlands stream. It's a fine walk for any time of the year and particularly on a midsummer's day when it's too hot to walk in the open.

The Woodcutter's Trail seems to have a number of variations, depending on who you speak to. This is mine.

Newlands Forest is the remains of a *buitepost* (outpost) of the Dutch East India Company. It was one of a number in the colony set up to provide timber for housing and ship repairs. This one was known as *Paradys* (Paradise), some say due to its close proximity to the fleshpots of Wijnberg and the Tap House at Driekoppen, the site of which is now occupied by a UCT residence.

Start from the parking area next to the main gates of Newlands Forest on Union Avenue. Walk through the gates to a T-junction before turning left, to reach Newlands Stream.

Then, follow the stream up along its right bank. Your aim is to follow the stream as high up as the path will allow, whilst not crossing over it.

The main population of the forest is made up of alien blue gums, pines and oaks. However, a fair bit of indigenous vegetation remains, with a surprisingly large number of wild peach trees (*Kiggelaria africana*). This particular species was declared the South African "Tree

of the Year" in 1996, and has an interesting story attached to it.

The wild peach tree plays host in summertime to armies of small black caterpillars. They strip the tree almost bare in a feeding frenzy and, when they have done, they "abseil" to the ground on a fine silk thread. They then march off to find a nearby suitable surface on which to attach themselves and pupate.

The pupae remain dormant until the next spring, and out comes your common black and orange butterfly (*Garden acraea*) seen in all Cape gardens. After mating the female butterfly carefully seeks out another wild peach tree and lays her eggs on the leaves. She is very fussy about where she lays her eggs, as the resultant caterpillars will not eat the leaves of any other tree.

I once had a large and healthy wild peach in my garden, but the consequent annual mess on the white walls of the house, where thousands of caterpillars had decided to winter in their unsightly cocoons, was just too much for me.

One day in fit of pique, I cut it down – tree of the bloody year or not. I still suffer from immense feelings of guilt about this and am considering a psychoanalyst.

The stump keeps looking at me.

For the rest of your walk through Hampton Court Maze/Newlands Forest . . . after reaching a gravel road, follow it back to Newlands stream, where you can descend down the opposite bank.

The walk should take about one-and-a-half hours.

Or several years if you get lost.

Cape Times, September 12, 1997

Up above Simon's Town

Gunshots and barking dogs

Gunshots and barking dogs are hardly what you would expect to hear on a walk through one of the most beautiful fynbos hot spots on the Peninsula. But that's almost a racing certainty when you do the walk to Grootkop, high above Simon's Town.

Don't be alarmed by either the gunshots or the dogs, or even that it's high above Simon's Town. Most of the work is done by your car, driving to the start at the top of Red Hill.

And both dogs and guns are well under control.

Klawer Valley, normally well hidden from the public glare, is in a large bowl above the charming olde worlde town.

It is Naval property and closed to the public, but clearly visible from Grootkop.

On the right-hand side of the valley can be seen ammunition silos and near the middle, a firing range, which will explain the alarming gunshots.

Bound to be answering the gunshots are the irritated pupils of the nearby dog school.

But the view from the top of Grootkop isn't all aggression. Right below you is tranquil Kleinplaas Dam – Simon's Town's main water supply. And on a clear day you can see Table Mountain, Constantiaberg and Chapman's Peak. Not to mention the other Grootkop between Hout Bay and Camps Bay.

It's a bit confusing having two Grootkops, but just imagine how many we'd have had if we'd won our bid for the Olympic Games!

Another view from this highest peak in the area is Seaforth, just peeping out.

To the left of that, among some trees, is Botha's Camp. This has nothing whatsoever to do with the finger wagging "Groot Krokodil". It's named after the South African training ship *General Botha* which was moored in Simon's Bay from 1922 until 1942.

She was there for the purpose of training young men for a career at sea as officers in the Merchant Navy. During the Second World War it was decided that she represented far too tempting a target for German submarines. So the entire operation was moved ashore to Red Hill.

In 1948 the college moved to

Gordon's Bay and the site left behind became known as Botha's Camp. I had the honour and privilege of being a "Bothy Boy" in 1957 and 1958. Many a name amongst seafaring men were Bothy Boys, including war heroes "Sailor" Malan and J C Nettleton, VC.

Alas, the college is no more, due to a lack of interest by South African youngsters in a seagoing career.

It was certainly a way of seeing the world, as I discovered by visiting 42 countries before I was out of my teens.

Today, with modern air travel, that seems like old hat.

Or is this just another old-timer, mumbling about the spirit of adventure missing in the youth of today?

Start the walk from the top of Red Hill on the M66 between Scarborough and Simon's Town.

It is about 100 metres beyond the sign of the grave of Just Nuisance (more about him in another column).

Allow two hours for the return trip of 5,4 km. If you take a dog, it must be on a lead, as you cross over private property.

For this reason you need permits from both the Simon's Town Municipality – phone (021) 786-1551 – and the Red Hill Landowners' Conservation Group – phone (021) 786-1620.

That may seem like a hassle, but believe me, just the fynbos makes it well worthwhile.

And, like the best things in life, it's free.

Cape Times, September 19, 1997

Chapman's contour path

Wrong prisoners, wrong war and wrong bloody pass as well!

If there's one thing that really gets up my nose, it's people who tell me with great conviction that Chapman's Peak Drive was built by Italian prisoners of war.

I know that's probably not important to most people but, horror of horrors, as a resident of Hout Bay I recently picked up a glossy and a very nicely put together publication called *Hout Bay Regional Property Guide*.

Dare I say that it was glossy enough to even look highly authoritative. Imagine how far my jaw dropped when I read the heading – "Some interesting facts about the area" – and it goes right in there, boots and all, and says: "Chapman's Peak Drive was built by Second World War Italian prisoners of war."

Well! I got my knickers in a right knot I can tell you. Wrong prisoners. Wrong war. And wrong bloody pass as well!

Saying it is one thing. Publishing it is an entirely different matter. If you do that often enough, an untruth becomes a truth.

You have literally rewritten history and made things happen which didn't. Ask the old Nat government. They were past masters at rewriting history to suit themselves.

The guilty party in this case call themselves Giraffe Publishing. As they don't appear to have their heads above the undergrowth of misinformation, perhaps a name change to Ostrich Publishing might be more appropriate.

But what about the walkers?

Now that I've got that off my chest, we can walk. (Read on for the real truth about Chapman's Peak Drive.)

This three-hour walk treats you to one of the most breathtaking views in the country. It's a one-way hike, so have someone pick you up at the end, or have a car waiting. Or a lot of excess energy.

The first half-hour is up a fairly steep ravine. Thereafter it's an easy walk, more or less on the level, dipping in and out of wooded ravines. The view of Hout Bay from on high is quite unforgettable.

But then it wasn't always this linguistic hybrid. Van Riebeeck called it "'t Hout Baeitjen" and English, French and Portuguese naviga-

tional charts followed suit with their versions of "Wood Bay", "Bay du Bois" and "Porto di Ligno".

But in 1607, before Van Riebeeck was even thought of, Captain David Middleton of the English ship *Consent* decided to send ashore the master's mate – one John Chapman – on a chancy mission into the bay to see if sheltered anchorage and fresh water were to be found. As no charts existed at the time, it was indeed chancy.

The bay was named Chapman's Chaunce (note the olde English spelling). The name was later relocated to the peak and the bay surrounding Noordhoek beach (Chapman's Bay), to become the oldest English name on the South African coast.

The hike begins at the last picnic area before reaching the top of Chapman's Peak Drive from the Hout Bay end. It ends at the car park 1,5 km from the Chapman's Peak Hotel, near the East Fort.

Oh! I nearly forgot. When Chapman's Peak Drive was built between 1915 and 1922 (partly during the First World War) it would have been difficult to use Italian prisoners of war. Mainly because they were on our side.

Prisoners were indeed used. But they were our very own convicts. The confusion no doubt arises from the fact that 5 000 Italian POWs were used to make a start on the Du Toit's Kloof Pass between 1943 and 1945.

Different prisoners. Different war. Different pass. And that is a *real* fact.

Cape Times, September 26, 1997

The Penguin Walk

Not the latest
dance step

It's not the latest dance step. The penguin walk is a delightful little doddle, just south of Simon's Town.

And you will be enchanted by these quaint little creatures with their comic appearance and gait. Heaven forbid, you might even allow an *Ag, shame* to pass your lips.

But when you get there, just a kilometre past Simon's Town Police Station, don't be surprised if you hear what sounds like donkeys "hee-hawing" in the coastal bush surrounding Seaforth and Boulders beach.

The donkeys are, in fact, jackass penguins, so named because of their call.

Despite the similarity of the raucous braying of a donkey and this particular penguin's call, ornithologists far prefer the name African penguin.

Rather surprisingly, they are the only penguins that breed on the whole of the African coastline. This particular corner of the continent seems to be top of the penguin pops at the moment, as their population has grown from one pair in 1985 to some 1 700 birds in just a decade.

Start the walk at Seaforth parking area and go past Foxy Beach to the Boulders. And if you're feeling really energetic, do the full 1,7 km-waddle (half an hour) to Froggy Pond. It's all on the level (and punctuated with lots of *Ag, shames*).

Underfoot, the walk couldn't be more varied – from tar road to neatly trimmed lawn, to soft sand and granite rocks.

Best leave Fido at home, though. Not because of the underfoot. Mainly because of the penguins. Dogs and penguins don't exactly hit it off together.

Fido would be a bit like a pork sausage in a synagogue here. Highly unpopular. Anyway, you won't get him past the entrance gate where you'll have to cough up R10 for adults and R1,50 for children.

The penguins are really worth the ten bucks – especially if you've learnt a little bit about them beforehand. F'rinstance, did you know they live up to 25 years and tend to remain faithful to their mate and breeding place for life?

Damn site better than some of us.

They are present in the Boulders Coastal Park throughout the year, with the highest numbers from February to April. The population is at its lowest from now until December.

As you see them here, they are not in their natural habitat. One could almost say they have been forcibly moved here by a sort of ornithological Group Areas Act. Normally they breed on the offshore rocky islands, which have built up layers of guano metres thick.

They would burrow out a nesting place horizontally in the guano. This must make them one of the few creatures that build their homes out of their own excrement.

However, when bird droppings were elevated in status from the unmentionable to being a valuable fertiliser, they lost their homes. As we have destroyed their natural habitat, they are now burrowing into soil.

The chicks, when hatched, are fed a regurgitated fish porridge by their parents. At about twelve weeks old they waddle down to the sea and swim off into the sunset.

They are now utterly alone and must support themselves – never having known what food looks like. Instinctively they have to recognise whole fish as food, and catch it. More than half of them fail the examination and die of starvation – simply because they can't see the food for the fish.

On your little waddle-doddle down Boulders way, whatever you do, don't touch the penguins. You could be fined up to R3 000 for wilfully disturbing them.

And if the authorities don't get you, the bird's powerful beak certainly will.

Cape Times, October 3, 1997

HEE-
HAW

The Echo Valley Double-Cross

Not your average Wild West movie

With the opening in October 1997 of the new cableway up Table Mountain, we can at last get to the Upper Cable Station again – the easy way. It will only take four minutes of your time but sixty smackeroos out of your pocket.

So you think that's a rip-off? Well, at a bit more than £6, you won't even get a round of drinks for that in the Old Country. Let alone the crowded tube train from Heathrow to central London.

We've been spoilt. That's the trouble with us. So, if you want one of the most spectacular rides in the world, then you must just *kak en betaal*, as my rather coarse friend Piet would say. (He comes from Kakamas, which apparently explains everything.)

The Front Table forms the well-known profile of Table Mountain. Behind it, and about 300 metres lower, is the Back Table, housing the five main reservoirs of Table Mountain. Separating the two is the deep Echo Valley.

One of my favourite walks I call the Echo Valley Double-Cross. This is not a Zane Gray novel or a sequel to *The Gunfight at OK Corral*. It's a nice hike. Somewhat strenuous and somewhat long (three to four hours), but full of fascination. Especially if you drop in at the Waterworks Museum along the way.

The trail winds its way along boardwalks and down long ladders to cross Echo Valley at its western end. It then follows a series of valleys with thought-provoking names: Ark Valley, Valley of Isolation and Valley of the Red Gods are all beautiful in their own way.

Table Mountain has five reservoirs on the Back Table, of which you will see the two main ones. Sandwiched between the two is the little known Waterworks Museum, documenting the history of the building of the dams more than a century ago. They even have an immaculate steam engine, which used to cart supplies from the old cableway at the top of Kasteels Poort to the dam sites. Coal was imported all the way from Wales to provide it with fuel on top of the mountain.

Here we are, a century later, with the biggest coal terminal in the world at Richard's Bay and we had to import coal from Wales! It

goes like that sometimes. Even if you are not a museum freak, this one is bound to have something to interest you, situated, as it were, at the coalface of Cape Town's early water supply.

A hundred years ago, when these dams were built, they provided the Mother City with its entire water supply. Today, if all five dams were full, they would run dry in just one week.

Makes you think. Where are we going to get the water in just twenty years from now when we keep adding to the population?

Return to the Upper Cable Station by re-crossing Echo Valley, this time at the eastern end. Try to suppress any urge to test the appropriateness of Echo Valley's name. Only Philistines do that.

This auditory version of a Narcissus complex simply adds to the noise pollution and irritates the hell out of fellow hikers.

Cape Times, October 10, 1997

The King's Blockhouse

Sip a gin and tonic
and think of England

God save the Queen! And the King. And the Prince of Wales. Well . . . He seems to have done quite a good job of saving their blockhouses, even though Charles continues to fall off ponies and ER II endures yet another *annus horribilis.*

There are cynics and anti-royalists out there who really believe that the trio of batteries on Devil's Peak will outlast the British monarchy. I must say, the King's Blockhouse on the ridge above Rhodes Memorial is in threateningly good nick.

But the Queen's Blockhouse and the Prince of Wales's Blockhouse just above De Waal Drive aren't in nearly such fine fettle. Every time Charles talks to a flower and Her Majesty says "On behalf of my husband and I . . ." another brick crumbles.

Why not take a walk this weekend to the King's Blockhouse? The view is a mind blow. And well it should be, considering its original purpose.

Officially known on survey maps as the King's Battery, it was built by the British during their first occupation of the Cape be-

tween 1795 and 1803. Its guns were never fired in anger. However, it was used to accommodate convict labour during the afforestation of Devil's Peak in the latter part of the nineteenth century.

The Prince of Wales and Queen's blockhouses were the other two of a trio of small forts built in 1797 to protect Cape Town against attack from the south – which is exactly the route the British themselves chose after the Battle of Muizenberg. They were not going to allow a repeat performance by an enemy.

Anyway, there they stand today, these relics of our history, in all their glory. Well – the King in all his glory, the Queen a bit jaded and the Prince totally knackered.

This easy little circular route, on which you will see all three, takes about an hour and fifteen minutes and covers just over three kilometres.

Start by driving to the very end of Tafelberg Road. That's exactly five kilometres past the Lower Cable Station (don't let them dare stop you. They've kept it closed for long enough!). One hundred metres beyond, where Tafelberg Road

comes to an end, is a stone and iron gate of some antiquity across the gravel road.

Walk through the gate into a grove of rather interesting trees. They are exotics and were obviously planted a long time ago. But what makes them interesting is that they have bark like a cork tree and acorns like an oak tree, but leaves unlike either. These apparent arboreal mongrels are called – not surprisingly – cork oaks.

Continue along the gravel road towards the King's Blockhouse which starts to peek out from above the skyline ahead.

Once at your destination, admire the superb view of the Mother City from this vantage point and see how well you know the various landmarks.

For the return journey, get to the reservoir above the blockhouse and follow the contour path back to the cork oaks and your car.

Go home. Pour a gin and tonic and drink a toast to the monarchy. Or just close your eyes and think of England . . .

Cape Times, October 17, 1997

Peers Cave

Visit to
an old resident's home

Quite a few people in Fish Hoek can remember the Second World War. One or two can even bring back memories of the Great Conflict of 1914-1918. But no one can quite recall the first resident of the seaside town.

That's because he moved into the neighbourhood about 30 000 years ago. And I can even give you his address. It was Peers Cave, off Ou Kaapseweg, Fish Hoek 7975. Not that there were any postal deliveries in those days.

Anthropologists from all over the world were all of a flutter in 1926 when Victor Peers and his son Bertie unearthed a skull in what was then called Skildersgat, the cave which now bears their name. The skull was identified by experts to be that of a thirty-year-old male about 1,67 metres tall. More importantly, he was estimated to have lived about 15 000 years ago. So really, he was very much the new kid on the block, living in a house his ancestors had occupied for 15 000 years before him. What excited the experts was that the Fish Hoek Man, as he became known, was different in many respects from his modern descendants.

Take a hike this weekend and check out the oldest abode on the block. And reflect on what the neighbourhood looked like thousands of years back when the sea filled this valley and the Southern Peninsula was an island.

The shoreline was just below. You might even pick up a few seashells and reflect even further on the food packaging used in those days, while you eat your sandwiches and have a cool drink from their very different containers. But don't *you* leave them lying around as well!

The cave is roughly 25 metres wide at the mouth and twelve metres deep. The ceiling averages six or seven metres above the uneven sandy floor.

To get to the start of the hike, drive down from the top of Ou Kaapseweg in a southerly direction. After a little over four kilometres, the first turn-off to the right is Silvermine Road, leading to Noordhoek. From this point, continue down Ou Kaapseweg for a further 500 metres. This will bring you to the crest of a hill where the

road bends to the right. On this bend there is a small parking area for about ten cars. Park here.

To the left of the parking area there is a metal boom with a sandy road leading off behind it. Follow this track and you will see the white trig (trigonometrical) beacon on top of Skilderskop directly ahead, giving away the position of Peers Cave below it.

You will come upon the cave quite suddenly when you are level with a point about 200 metres beyond the beginning of the sand in the valley below.

At one stage a few years ago, this cave, a valuable archeological site, was covered in mindless graffiti. It seems that its original Afrikaans name of Skildersgat (Painters' Cave) was taken literally.

It was painstakingly cleaned and restored to its natural condition in about 1994 but, unfortunately, it also lost its original Khoi paintings.

It saddens me greatly to see that these sick people with their public-toilet mentality are once again fouling the mountain with their graffiti presence.

Johan, Herman and Ibrahim, my message to you, and all those like you, is go and seek help. You need it.

The Shipwreck Trail

A little something
on the beach

"Little Tommy Tucker sang for his supper . . ." as the nursery rhyme goes. But this one didn't sing as much as let out a heart-rending groan as she hit the rocks just south of Olifantsbos, in the Cape of Good Hope Nature Reserve.

It was 1942 and we were at war with the Third Reich. A glamorous version of the ignominious end of the *Thomas T. Tucker* is that she was attempting to avoid the unwelcome attentions of a U-boat. Considering she was carrying a cargo of tanks at the time, the U-boat story makes sense.

But, according to at least one maritime historian, the end of Tommy Tucker was probably just plain bad navigation. Make sure you navigate your way safely around the Shipwreck Trail near Cape Point.

This is a two-hour, 5,8-km walk with a tasty sprinkling of history and nature. Apart from the *Thomas T. Tucker* another shipwreck, the *Nolloth,* lies at her final resting place a few hundred metres further on.

This Dutch coaster, wrecked in 1965, was carrying a large cargo of liquor. When the news got out, she attracted droves of people hopeful of picking up a little something on the beach.

Alas, the Department of Customs and Excise had arrived first and set up camp. I always did hate them. Especially when they used to ask me: "Did you got any magazines?" (Nudge, nudge. Wink, wink. Say no more.) With the emphasis on magazines. Not on grammar.

I was never once asked if I had any cocaine or heroin. Only pornographic literature. As if that was going to single-handedly destroy the country – so to speak.

But shipwrecks are far from being the only interesting things on this delightful circular trail starting and ending at Olifantsbos.

At the start, you might well see a herd of bontebok, which seem to be happiest around the parking area. The reason for their preference for this specific area is that it used to be a farm, which as a result of the farming activity reverted to grassland. This is exactly what they want. As their natural habitat is Bredasdorp, where there is much more grass in the vegetation tapes-

try, this little spot seems like a home from home.

Also close to the parking area is the largest stand of wild dagga (*Leonotis leonurus*) I have ever seen. Its bright orange flowers during the summer and autumn months cannot be missed.

But before all my Rastafarian readers go rushing out there – read on, mon.

It's not narcotic and is no relation to dagga (*cannabis*). It does, however, have a wide range of uses in medicine, with extracts curing everything from coughs to skin complaints.

On your way to Tommy Tucker you are bound to see something very rare. Contradictory as that may seem, the African black oystercatcher is quite common here.

These distinctive birds have bright red legs, beak and eye rings contrasting with black plumage. They are one of the world's rarest oystercatchers and have a global population of only about 5 000. Despite their rarity, you are certain to encounter them.

From now until March is their breeding season – they are extremely vocal in defence of eggs or chicks and will not hesitate to tell you off and try to lead you away from their offspring.

It is important that you comply, because as long as they are trying to lure you away, their eggs or chicks are exposed to predators.

It's bad enough being rare – but exposed as well is a bit too much!

Cape Times, October 31, 1997

Frontal contour path

Mother Mountain was
six times her present height

Take a walk between the table legs this weekend and marvel at the Mother City below your feet. Not to mention that which towers majestically above you. The frontal contour path traverses Table Mountain from one end to the other, along its base, without demanding too much effort. Except at the start, that is, when you need to get up to the cliff face. Then it's a cakewalk, and it starts on the second hairpin bend above Kloof Nek.

The route takes you under the new cableway and into the pleasant and shady Silverstream Ravine, worthy of a tea break, just before your zigzag descent back down to Tafelberg Road.

Mother Mountain is a wondrous thing. Its rocks are about 600 million years old, but as a raised geological feature, Table Mountain is only a maximum of 60 million years old, compared to the age of the planet, which is 4 600 million years.

The age of Table Mountain may be difficult to imagine, but it is easier to comprehend major events in relation to one another, if we concertina these 4 600 million years into one calendar year.

- During all of January and half of February, Earth supports no life at all. It is an inorganic planet in the process of cooling.
- On about 17 February simple microbes form.
- On 4 March the earliest known sedimentary rocks form.
- On 3 September the continents start drifting apart.
- On 13 November animals evolve hard shells.
- On 29 November vertebrates evolve and earth is clothed in plant life.
- On 7 December coal is deposited.
- On 15 December oxygen reaches present levels.
- On 22 December dinosaurs rule the earth.
- On 25 December a cataclysmic event causes the extinction of many species including the dinosaurs (an unfortunate choice of dates).
- On 26 December, the precursor of Table Mountain is formed – *at least six times its present height.*
- On 31 December at ten pm

primitive man first sets foot on the planet. Christ is born at fourteen seconds to midnight and the Industrial Revolution begins a second before the year ends. Immense geological changes take place on the last day of our compressed year. As recently as four minutes to the stroke of midnight on 31 December, the whole of False Bay is dry land.

If all of this makes you feel totally insignificant in The Greater Scheme of Things, then you need to do this walk. Just to get things back on the level. To wish yourself Happy New Year. And to enjoy the breathtaking panorama of the City Bowl and beyond. Marvel at the new cable car as it passes overhead, slowly revolving on its own axis. (Well at least the floor revolves. That's the same thing, isn't it?)

The ravine up which it travels on its four-minute journey to the top is called India Ravine. For years I imagined it had something to do with being a halfway house to India, or suchlike. No such romantic stuff at all. Quite simply, viewed from the city, it looks like the map of India. And Africa Ravine to the left of it, with a tad more imagination, looks like home.

Cape Times, November 7, 1997

Camps Bay–
Green Point contour

What's in a name?

Imagine if you and your beloved lived in upmarket Clifton and were referred to by officialdom as "a scum of a cobbler and his cross-grained slut of a wife". Harsh words indeed. But it happened.

The insult is contained in Adam Tas's diary of 1697 and refers to Jacobus Schoenmaker and his wife. The original name of this delightful gem of coastal suburbs – perhaps the most beautiful of all South Africa's coastal towns – was Schoenmakersgat. Not very beautiful. And such a nice place.

Jacobus the cobbler gave Clifton its first name. It almost certainly got its present name a century ago, from the owner of the original Clifton Hotel – Mrs Bess Clifton.

This is just one of the stunning views you will get from the immensely rewarding walk from Camps Bay to Green Point, on a path just above the building line.

Only the first five minutes of this less-than-two-hours' walk require any effort. The rest is a delightfully scenic stroll, mostly on the level, overlooking our captivating Sunset Coast. Lion's Head towers above you with brooding grandeur.

I am reminded of Rio de Janeiro and the view of Copacabana from Corcovado. It might well be concrete, but it does have a certain magnetism.

Your first views on this walk, however, are not of concrete suburbia but of the most amazing concentration of Watsonias which have sprung up with a vengeance since the devastating fire of 1995.

Then look over the famous Clifton beaches, come uncomfortably close to the mansions of upper Fresnaye, look down on the flatland of Sea Point and finally onto the green sportsfield of Green Point Common. A rewarding walk without too much effort, but you will need a car at each end or someone to pick you up at a pre-arranged time.

Start at the hairpin bend on the road from Kloof Nek to Clifton. The route ends at the very top of Glengariff Road, Three Anchor Bay, where it joins the beginning of Springbok Road.

Along the way, notice the two entirely different types of rock forming the main mass of Lion's Head.

The granite base is igneous in origin, having been pushed up from below the earth's crust. The overlying sandstone which forms Lion's Head itself, however, is sedimentary in origin. That is to say it was formed from above, with layer upon layer of sediment dropping out onto the beds of ancient seas and rivers.

You are looking at a history book of the planet.

The Atlantic suburbs took a long time to be developed. Van Riebeeck and his successors were far more drawn to the fertile ground surrounding the Liesbeek River. They were interested in vegetables, not vistas.

The names of other places to be seen on this walk have also under-gone an interesting metamorphosis over the years. Camps Bay was named after Frederich von Camptz, described by the governor in the 1780s as a "troublesome and annoying person". At least he didn't seem to have a cross-grained slut of a wife, which I suppose was a blessing.

He owned a farm in the area and it became known as Von Camptz Baai. Property developers around 1900 called it New Brighton before the original name was anglicised to Camps Bay.

Old Frederich would have been far less troublesome if he'd had any idea of what his land was going to be worth 200 years later.

Cape Times, November 14, 1997

Cape of Good Hope hiking trail

Everything from bontebok to baboons

In November 1997 we did a sort of Two Oceans marathon. Well, it was not quite a marathon, but it was two oceans. You could say it was the hikers' version of the same thing.

The Cape of Good Hope Nature Reserve gives you everything from bontebok to baboons, from wide-open plains to cliff-hanging contours.

And what's more, this two-day, overnight trail is just around the corner. That is, if you live in the southern suburbs.

From behind the Boerewors Curtain it's a bit further, but still only an hour and a half from home.

So get yourself down to where the oceans meet at Cape Point and enjoy this many-faceted mother of a trail.

It's not easy. So if you're not a regular hiker, stop reading. But it is an exciting and varied challenge.

Day one is the day of the open plains. It begins at the main gate and travels down the Atlantic Coast to Cape Point and the overnight hut.

There are snowfields of everlastings and a blazing forest of yellow pincushion proteas. Nature paints the rocks with splashes of bright orange-red lichen, as if a graffiti vandal had been let loose. But it is God's paintbrush that has been used.

For this fynbos beauty, you have to pay a price. The cost is more than 23 km and nine hours. Unless, of course, you miss out the best part, and take a short cut, reducing the exchange rate to nineteen kilometres and seven hours.

Either way, it's a long day.

I'm ashamed to admit, we took the short cut. I hang my head. But otherwise, heaven forbid, we would have missed the start of the rugby test against the French. (On a tiny portable battery-powered TV with a screen all of 75 x 50 mm.) Imagine three intense retired rugger-bugers huddled together trying to focus on this minute screen.

Some things *are* more important than hiking. And we won!

Somewhere along the hike, you are bound to run into wildlife.

Not if, but when, you encounter baboons, please DO NOT feed them, under any circumstances.

You will be signing their death

warrant. Feed baboons and they will come to expect it. Don't feed them and you could be attacked for not doing what they have come to expect.

Attacks on humans not playing the game will follow your feeding them, as surely as the next step – a game ranger's bullet.

Think about that the next time you feel the urge to feed a baboon.

Ag shame! Yes, indeed.

Day two is the day of the stunning cliffside views. If day one was long and flat, the return route up the False Bay coast is quite the opposite.

A relatively short eleven kilo-metres is made much longer by the undulating route along the cliff edge which overlooks False Bay far below.

This is not a hike for occasional day trippers out of trim. But it is a trail for the dedicated hiker who hasn't done it before.

Add this one to your sleeve. It's a must.

But be warned. The terrain is tough underfoot and there is barely a drop of water along the entire route.

So good boots and two litres of water are the order of the day.

Cape Times, November 21, 1997

The Stinkwood Trail, Kirstenbosch

In the botanical treasure house of the world

What could be more Scottish than bagpipes, whisky and heather? The Scots are particularly proud of their heather and put pictures of it everywhere, including on whisky bottles.

In all of Europe there are 21 species of *Erica* heath. We in the Western Cape have 657 and counting. Such a huge variety is unequalled by any other plant group in the world.

And it's all in our tiny corner of the African continent. Which makes one look afresh at places such as the Kirstenbosch National Botanical Gardens, the administrative capital of the Cape floral kingdom.

The botanical world is divided into six so-called "floral kingdoms". The largest in size is the Boreal kingdom which covers most of the northern hemisphere and takes up 42% of the world's land mass.

The richest by far, in terms of the concentration of an immensely wide variety of species, is the Cape floral kingdom. This stretches along a narrow coastal strip from Clanwilliam in the north to Cape Town and east as far as Grahamstown. It occupies a paltry 0,4% of the world's land-mass, yet has the highest concentration of flowering plants on the planet, despite being the smallest in size.

We are living in the botanical treasure house of the world. Go to Kirstenbosch and have a look at it. The plants of the Western Cape are remarkably different from plants found anywhere else in the world – and more than two thirds of them are found nowhere else.

A good place to begin discovering the botanical treasure trove in our own backyard is on the short 1,3-km circular Stinkwood Trail, in the heart of Kirstenbosch. It will take a mere forty minutes, but requires a bit of effort climbing some long steps on the outward journey. The modest entrance fee is more than compensated for by the thought of bacon and eggs and all the trimmings in the restaurant, to be enjoyed after you have worked up an appetite.

Once through the turnstiles simply follow the signposts indicating the Stinkwood Trail, past the Nature Study School and eventually up some log steps into a forest glade

called, rather ominously, "Donkergat".

You will soon reach an enormous dead pine tree. It has clearly been "ring barked" in order to kill it, as it is very much an invasive alien in this indigenous forest. "Ring barking", or cutting through the bark in a complete ring around the base of a tree, has the same effect as if you were to punch holes in a straw.

One minute's walk after the dead pine, you will reach a gravel road. This is your highest point. While catching your breath and thinking about the smell of bacon and eggs, notice a tree, like many others, with a plastic name plate on it. The early Dutch settlers had some pretty indelicate names for certain plants, such as the strong-smelling *paardepis*.

But this particular nameplate has always rather tickled me. There's nothing unusual about the common turkey berry tree, except its Afrikaans name. *Gewone bokdrol* describes its fallen berries perfectly. The gravel road now tumbles down the slope rather steeply until the smell of breakfast renders the signposts totally unnecessary. Just follow your nose.

Cape Times, November 28, 1997

Sandy Bay

Not for voyeurs
or Mother Grundies

Even without the nudists, believe it or not, this is an interesting walk. But if you have a problem with nudity, or if you only want to walk across Sandy Bay to ogle, then it's best you stay home. Neither Mother Grundies nor voyeurs are welcome on this nearly three-hour return voyage to some interesting shipwrecks.

Crossing Sandy Bay on a hot day over a weekend, dressed in mountain boots and backpack, you might feel the need to stare blankly at the sand one metre directly ahead of you as you walk. This way, you'll avoid feeling awkward about being overdressed.

On the other hand it might be easier to take off all your clothes and put them on again once you are at the other end of the beach.

However, I will *not* share with you what a friend said when seeing me dressed in mountain boots and a backpack and absolutely nothing else. I was quite hurt actually. And I don't see what an old-fashioned petrol pump has to do with it anyway.

Entirely on the level, this walk starts at the southern end of Llandudno along an extremely well-trodden path, crosses Sandy Bay beach and then dives into the bushes and continues parallel to the coast.

About half an hour after leaving the bare bods behind, the rocky peninsula of Oudeschip presents you with three fascinating shipwrecks. And the most fascinating of them all, you can't see.

It's inside. Not on top.

The wreck of the *Maori* lies some way beneath the surface, just below your vantage point. This British steamship struck these rocks just after midnight on 5 August 1909. Only 22 of the 53 crew lived to tell the tale of what has been described as the most dramatic rescue by rocket apparatus ever carried out on the South African coast.

As it had taken 48 hours to transport the rocket apparatus to the rescue scene, it was decided to build a rocket station to house rescue equipment to avert another disaster.

Wrong.

The rocket station, built in 1913, still stands at the top of the hill, empty and useless. Nobody told them that lightning never strikes in

the same place twice.

Helicopters have long since taken the place of firing a line-carrying rocket over a stricken vessel.

The other two more obvious disasters are the *Boss 400* and the *Harvest Capella.*

The latter was a "long-liner" which used, instead of nets, long lines with hooks every few metres to fish for hake. This way they avoided bruising the fish and could get up to three times the price by flying them fresh to Spain. *Harvest Capella* stopped long-lining and high-flying rather abruptly in 1986.

The *Boss 400*, a floating crane, came to grief in June 1994 in driving rain and gale-force winds.

The eighteen crew were all lifted to safety by helicopter under the watchful eye of the obsolete rocket station.

Whilst walking this 6,8-km (return) trail, keep your eye on the boulders and not the bods.

Cape Times, December 5, 1997

Orange Kloof

A wilderness
within a city

For more than sixty years this has been the Mother City's best-kept secret.

Apart from the fact we didn't stand a snowball's of winning the Olympic bid.

The Orange Kloof Amphitheatre in the upper reaches of the Hout Bay valley has for many years been an enigma to some and a source of irritation to others.

An irritation, as only the privileged and best-connected were allowed entry. And an enigma because one wasn't supposed to know too much about it anyway.

It's been that way for the entire life of most Capetonians. Now all that has changed – paradise has been opened.

But hang on. Don't go rushing off as if gold had just been panned in the upper reaches of the Disa River. Entry is strictly by permit and is issued on the basis that you are a part of a group of twelve people (maximum) for the purpose of environmental education.

And you need to be led by an environmental education officer, who will tell you all about the birds and the bees.

This is a special experience – a wilderness within a city.

For three generations there have been stringent fire protection measures to keep the public out of this arboreal Jurassic Park. Only since 1996 has it been possible to step back in time and walk through indigenous forest that is essentially the same as it was many centuries ago.

This is an educational experience in an outdoor laboratory. It's an eerie experience seeing the forest as van Riebeeck did, when he wrote in his diary that *"'t Hout Baaitjen* had the finest forests in all the world"*.

A five-year plan is being implemented to remove the pine and gum plantations and return the soil to its rightful and regal owners – the silver trees and yellowwoods of this, the richest floral kingdom on earth.

A number of different hikes are possible. The main circuit takes three hours along a gently sloping gravel ring road, with shorter guided hikes starting from the Environmental Education Centre.

If time allows, try to persuade

your guide to take you to Hell's Gates – one of the most beautiful waterfall ravines I have ever seen.

The amazing thing is that it took me half a century to discover this gem, barely three kilometres from where I live.

The reason this wilderness within a city has been closed to the public for three generations of hikers has been a fear bordering on paranoia that fire (more often than not caused by people) would destroy those trees that were left after a devastating fire in the area in 1933.

Thanks to the forest's amazing recovery and the enlightened thinking of the authorities, permits are now issued, but strictly for environmental education excursions.

Important indigenous trees to be found include silver trees, Cape beech (boekenhout) wild peach, yellowwood, red alder (rooiels), wild olive, assegaai, hard pear and milkwood.

To book, call (021) 689-7438 or (021) 713-0260. Dogs would be overwhelmed by the choice of trees and are not allowed.

Cape Times, December 12, 1997

Cobra Camp

Snakes
in perspective

Who's afraid of the big bad snake? Just about everyone, it seems. And it's so unfair! These victims of prejudice must be among the most maligned creatures on earth. Yet without them our gardens would be one big molehill and we could look forward to being ankle deep in rats. Take your choice. But more of the sinless serpent or vicious viper debate later.

Cobra Camp above Kommetjie is one place you are unlikely to encounter the little darlin's. Mainly because the route is along a broad Jeep track and the object of your fear is likely to have picked up your vibrations long before your arrival and slithered off into the bush.

Unless it's a puff adder. That's the one I worry about. Only because he doesn't flee at the first sign of your approach. His form of defence isn't retreat, it's camouflage. Brilliant camouflage. And he figures if he stays put and remains dead still you won't see him – especially in mottled shade. He's quite right, of course – unless you stand on him.

Then he's *your* problem.

I found that out a few weeks ago in the De Hoop Nature Reserve near Bredasdorp. The South African Athletics Association would have been proud of me. I think I came close to both the long jump and high jump records simultaneously. I also used a very naughty word and had to apologise to the ladies present. They were most understanding and said I didn't have to wash my mouth out with soap.

That was a relief, I can tell you.

But back to Cobra Camp. This easy two-hour five-kilometre return walk along a sandy Jeep track to an abandoned Second World War radar station is an utter delight.

You will walk past some absolutely classic fynbos and be further rewarded with a stunning view, looking down onto Kommetjie and the Slangkop lighthouse. Return via the same route, after exploring the three old blockhouses, each with a different vista. The place has an aura of history and mystery about it.

To find the start of this walk, get to the Ocean View township on the

Fish Hoek-Kommetjie road and turn left at the sign to Scarborough. Exactly two kilometres from the turnoff, on the crest of the hill, is a gate on the right marking the start of your amble through the fynbos.

And for heaven's sake – stop worrying about the snakes! While the danger of a small number of snake species must never be underestimated, I do believe that the threat of death from snakebite while out walking on the mountain should be put firmly in perspective.

In South Africa an average of fifteen people die each year as a result of snake bites. Eleven of these occur in northern KwaZulu-Natal. That leaves four for the rest of the country. By comparison more than 200 people are struck dead every year by lightning. Ten thousand people die in the carnage on our roads and 29 000 die as a result of smoking-related diseases.

So if *you* are a smoker, you can stop worrying about being bitten by a dangerous snake. What you are doing is 2 000 times more likely to kill you! They say there are two kinds of people who don't smoke. Non-smokers and rehabilitated smokers. I fall into the latter category which I'm told is a pain in the butt.

Here endeth the lesson.

Cape Times, December 19, 1997

Silvermine Reservoir

Canada
in the Cape

The inviting and unmistakable aroma of boerewors braaing over red-hot coals seems to hang quite comfortably in the still clean air of this Canadian lake.

The mountain backdrop and the pine forest are reflected perfectly in the mirror-smooth water. It would not be surprising to see a lumberjack in tartan shirt or Mountie on horseback emerge from the forest.

Actually it would. Because this Canadian lake happens to lie between Hout Bay and Muizenberg, on the Silvermine Plateau, in the good ol' R of SA.

In fact "boerie" with a Canadian backdrop goes down particularly well, especially when washed down with a couple of bitterly cold Castles.

Braaivleis, sunny skies and . . . a little walk in the forest. This one is for those hikers with a greater leaning towards the end of the walk than the beginning.

But the walk around the Silvermine Reservoir is really no hardship at all. At just over a kilometre on the level, it's a doddle. And you can pretend you're in Canada in midsummer (no icebergs).

If you get there early enough you can lay claim to one of the better "braaiplekkies" on the northern shore, close to the water, and in the most tranquil of surroundings.

The reservoir was built exactly a century ago, in 1898, by the old Kalk Bay municipality, to supply water for its residents. However, as that local authority has long since been swallowed up by big brother, it is now used solely for the purpose of watering the Westlake golf course.

Forget about looking for any silver. The name "Silvermine" is a complete misnomer. Although shafts were sunk in the area between 1675 and 1685 at the behest of the "Here XVII", not one ounce of silver was ever found.

The only silver now is in the cash till at the entrance gate. To gain entrance you will need to part with a few rands worth of it. (R4,00 per vehicle and R2,00 per person.)

The little "okes" under five are free and the old wrinklies get in for R1,50.

To get there, drive to the top of

Ou Kaapseweg and from the direction of Cape Town turn right into the Silvermine Nature Reserve.

After parting with your silver, follow the tarred road straight ahead for 2,4 km until you reach a parking area just to the right of the reservoir wall. Take the path to the top edge of the reservoir wall. You should be able to walk along the full length of the wall, to the other side of the reservoir. It has railings and is perfectly safe, but if you don't fancy this, or the walkway gate is locked, follow the road below the reservoir wall.

Either way, at the far end of the wall, turn right and walk along the water's edge amongst the stone fireplaces. (The nicer and shadier braaivleis spots are on the other side.)

Don't allow yourself to wander more than ten metres away from the water's edge, otherwise you will find yourself on the wrong path that goes past a stone public toilet.

As long as you stick as close as possible to the water's edge you will soon come to a concrete footbridge crossing over the narrow far end of the reservoir. With a little bit of planning there will be a roaring fire and an ice-cold beer waiting for you on the home stretch.

Cape Times, January 16, 1998

Newlands Forest

A taste of paradise
and a touch of history

"If you go down to the woods today, you're sure of a big surprise." Not the teddy bears' picnic mind you, but perhaps just a little taste of paradise.

Newlands Forest used to be known as *Paradys* in the days when it was a *buitepos* (outpost) of the Dutch East India Company. Some outpost. And not exactly your regular idea of paradise.

Life for the enlisted men of the VOC was far from heavenly. They had to put up with poor pay, poor rations and brutal discipline.

But for many who enlisted for service in Amsterdam, the alternative was too dreadful to contemplate – starvation in the economically depressed cities and countryside of Europe.

How the tables have turned. Newlands forest has a myriad of paths to offer, so have a set plan, otherwise you could finish up wandering around in ever-diminishing circles until the unmentionable happens.

One of my favourite walks is to explore the lower reaches of the forest to some ruins, rather erroneously known as Lady Anne Barnard's Cottage.

The route is mostly on level ground and in shade. Pleasant views accompany this easy walk, with a dash of history.

The cottage – or rather the ruins of it – was the master woodcutter's house. He was the official responsible for protecting the timber resources on Table Mountain. Apart from his own family and a slave (it was no paradise for him either), a small garrison of soldiers was based here.

In the late 1790s, with the Cape under British rule, the cottage was used briefly as a weekend getaway by Lady Anne Barnard and her husband Andrew, the deputy colonial secretary.

She must have been quite something, our Lady Anne, because nobody ever talks about *him* 200 years down the line. Because of her description of *Paradys* in her diary, the site became known – rather inappropriately – as Lady Anne Barnard's cottage.

Have a look at what's left of it and imagine life, if you can, without the noise of the nearby traffic. Yes, it could be paradise.

Start alongside the M3 freeway

into town, immediately after the traffic lights, where it crosses Newlands Avenue and Rhodes Drive. A concrete path runs parallel to the freeway, which you need to leave after about 150 metres, to dive into the forest.

There are so many paths in paradise, that trying to describe them can become somewhat hellish. Left, right, left, left, knit one, purl one, drop one . . .

So what if you get lost? In paradise it's a pleasure. And there's always the distant traffic noise to use as a homing beacon.

Cape Times, January 23, 1998

Take 100 steps to the shrine

Treat it with respect

This has got to be the shortest walk I have ever written about. In fact, it's only 100 steps – all of them up – and the same 100 steps back down again.

I had often seen people setting off on this little walk to I knew not where. The other day, after 25 years of watching people heading off up the mountain from the coastal road just beyond Bakoven, my curiosity finally got the better of me. I had, after all, driven past this spot at least 10 000 times; so a little look-see was well overdue.

Exactly two kilometres south of the Bakoven bus terminus are some steps ascending through a forest of spider gum – a rather unwelcome invader from Australia. Even in the pitch dark you would know it was from Oz – for the gums are members of the genus *Eucalyptus* – and the smell is heavy in the air as you climb the steps through the forest.

At the end is almost an oriental version of a Hansel and Gretel cottage in the forest. It's a Muslim shrine. The Holy Shrine of Sheikh Nurul Mubeen, who was laid to rest here in 1713.

He and others from the Dutch-colonised Indonesian Archipelago were brought here as political exiles and even as slaves. It is through them that there is Islam in South Africa. The learned sheikh was held captive on Robben Island, giving it a far longer history as an island penitentiary than most people imagine. He escaped and lived in this inaccessible place, from time to time hiding other spiritual leaders away from the Dutch colonists.

Over the years a number of these shrines sprang up, honouring Islamic leaders. They form a circle around the Cape Peninsula, appearing near Bakoven, on Robben Island, in Constantia, Vredehoek, Signal Hill and Simon's Town. No calamity, it is believed, will befall the land within that circle. Spiritual protection for Islam is ensured.

But should you decide to let your curiosity lead you up those steps it took me 25 years to climb, then remember one thing only – this is *Wakaf* ground – holy ground. It belongs to Allah. Treat it with respect.

Cape Times, June 2, 1995

Kakapo beach walk

Dry feet
and a red face

Imagine the captain's embarrassment. He's sailing this brand-new ship on its maiden voyage from England to New Zealand. Proud as punch, he must have been. She'd just left Table Bay a couple of hours earlier, on a foul and stormy night in May 1900. The Old Man, as the captain is known in maritime circles, mistook Chapman's Peak for Cape Point and did a sharp left turn.

To put it mildly, that was an unfortunate turn of events.

With engines at full-ahead and the assistance of a following gale-force wind as well as a spring tide, the ship was driven so high and dry onto the beach between Kommetjie and Noordhoek that the crew were able to walk off at low tide without getting their feet wet.

Try explaining that one to the ship's owners and cargo underwriters back in London. Not easy.

Go and see the wreck of the *Kakapo* on Long Beach. It's just 45 minutes along the sand from Kommetjie. Along the way you will be accompanied by the cry of gulls and the crash of the waves.

At the beginning of the walk you wouldn't be blamed for thinking you were in Arniston, with its quaint thatched and whitewashed cottages. The architectural style is so "Cape beach" that it almost begs to adorn a calendar.

Start from the parking area at the end of Kirsten Avenue in Kommetjie, and try to choose low tide for the walk, as the going is much easier on the firm sand of the intertidal zone.

After 45 minutes of walking in the direction of Hout Bay, seen nestling in the distance, you will come to the wreck. It is amazingly well preserved for its age. Notice how the rudder is still in the "hard-a-port" position, as a lasting reminder of the moment nearly a century ago when the captain desperately tried to correct his unfortunate error.

Too late, the maiden cried.

Why, you might ask, didn't he take any notice of the Kommetjie Lighthouse? Well, mainly because it wasn't there. More correctly known as the Slangkop Lighthouse, it was only built some years later.

After a series of shipwrecks in the area including the *Kakapo* and

the *Maori*, it was decided to build a lighthouse right on the spot where the *Clan Munro* met her end.

It was completed in 1914, just days before the outbreak of "The War to end all Wars".

This provided the authorities with a dilemma; for right next door was a military radio station, built in 1910.

To light the lamp of this spanking new lighthouse would have perfectly pinpointed a military target. So there stood this non-shin-

ing edifice, utterly useless.

It must have been the world's first non-illuminating lighthouse.

The lamp was finally lit in March 1919.

You can choose either to be drawn back towards it (45 minutes return) or continue to the end of the beach at Noordhoek (another 45 minutes). Hope someone will be there to pick you up, otherwise it's a long Long Beach.

Cape Times, February 6, 1998

St James coastal walk

A stroll
down memory lane

Some walks are said to be so easy that even octogenarians get fun out of them. You might well see the odd eighty-year-old on this delightful stroll along the seaside. But on the St James coastal walk I've even seen an "oxygenarian".

So help me, there was this dude with a walking stick and a nurse wheeling a bottle of oxygen.

Easier than that you simply do not get.

Mind you, it wasn't all that easy for him. He had to keep up with the oxygen bottle. Being dragged along by a plastic umbilical is not fun if you're not up to it.

But he was probably getting an immense amount of pleasure out of just remembering when . . .

Remembering when this was Cape Town's Golden Mile – the coastal stretch between Muizenberg and St James railway stations – wedged between mountain and sea.

Remembering when the St James Hotel was a private mansion called La Rivage. When the largest home along the route, the grand old, green-tiled "Graceland", was built for well-known merchant John Garlick.

And when Count Labia built his official residence as Italy's diplomatic representative to South Africa, in fine Venetian style.

Not to mention mining magnate and politician Sir Abe Bailey, architect *extraordinaire* Sir Herbert Baker, and pioneer of the Dutch Reformed Church the Reverend Andrew Murray, who all lived here at one time or another.

And with an extra puff of oxygen he might even tell you about empire builder Cecil John Rhodes who thought the "iodised salts" from the sea would benefit his ailing health. He was at the tender age of 44 when he bought his cottage-by-the-sea, right here along this walk.

Just four years later his failing health got the better of him and he died in the front bedroom of the cottage.

So much for iodised salts.

This charming coastal crawl is full of interesting local history, as well as rock pools and colourful bathing boxes. It starts on the seaward side of Muizenberg railway station and follows a concrete walkway along the water's edge,

ending at St James railway station.

The classic station building at Muizenberg was completed in 1913 and is today a national monument.

Along the way rough seas at high tide could result in a premature shower in places, so time your dash carefully. If you do want to get wet there are a couple of delightful tidal pools. The route takes you between picturesque beach huts that are often the subject of colourful postcards.

You could stroll back along Main Road, on the other side of the railway line, to get a closer look at some of the grand old homes that grace the route.

Or you could even catch the train back – if your oxygen has run out.

Cape Times, February 13, 1998

The Cat Walk

No dogs
allowed

It comes as no surprise that dogs are not allowed on the Cat Walk – that leisurely stroll along the salty promenade between Fish Hoek beach and Sunny Cove railway station. But a confrontation between canine and feline is not the issue – for there are no cats.

It's more a matter of that dreadful moment when a warm feeling between the toes is recognised for what it really is. Strictly no dogs allowed. Not even on a leash.

But then why the Cat Walk, if there are no cats either? And, for that matter, it's hardly even a walk – only 500 metres and ten minutes one way. But it's a delightful 500 metres which you can string out to half an hour, sitting on strategically placed benches along the way to enjoy the views.

Gaze across False Bay to the Hottentots Holland Mountains, stretching all the way to Cape Hangklip. It's even worth the odd swim here and there. Rock pools will provide fascination for young and old alike.

Oh, all right then – take an hour. And then there's always the return journey to enjoy.

At the end of the shoreline stroll, but before Sunny Cove station, is a whale-viewing point. This is not much cop at present, but during spring and early summer you will be treated to the wonderful spectacle of southern right whales breaching and cavorting just offshore.

When you see a southern right whale, the size of ten elephants, breaching, you have witnessed one of nature's spectacular events.

"Breaching" is when they jump almost clear of the water and come crashing down on their sides. Exactly why they do this is uncertain. Whale expert Dr Peter Best believes it is sheer exuberance. Other possibilities are communication in bad weather or a sign of aggression between males. The most unlikely theory is the removal of parasites.

But back to the Cat Walk, which is defined as a narrow raised path or, more recently, as a narrow platform used in fashion shows. That figures.

It's the main reason people sit on the benches. Not to rest, but to admire the passing parade.

Although everyone in Fish Hoek

knows it as the Cat Walk, it's more historically correct to call it the Jager Walk, so named after twelve-times mayor of the town, Herman Scott Jager.

For many years, one of Fish Hoek's main attractions has been the rocky coastline at the southern end of the bay. After the railway line was built in 1890, the difficulty of negotiating the rough and tumbled boulders was overcome by using the railway line as a means of access.

This was a fairly hazardous way of getting to your favourite fishing spot if you didn't have a timetable in your pocket – other than one for the tides.

So in 1931, the village manage-ment board decided to build a cement path along the rocky coastline. It was eventually completed in 1933, at what was then considered an enormous cost. In the pounds sterling of the day it amounted to R1 430, which caused an uproar in the village.

I still cause an uproar whenever I walk into a liquor store and tell the young assistant I can remember when Tassenberg was eighteen cents a bottle.

Oh, well. It's all relative, I suppose. Anyone who can remember that far back should stick to the Cat Walk and forget the peaks.

Cape Times, February 20, 1998

Kleinplaas dam

The ghost of
Just Nuisance

This two-and-a-quarter-hour return walk to Simon's Town's water supply, high above the town, could really suit your dog – mainly because it's along a fairly level Jeep track all the way.

But Pooch must be on a leash at all times. Not only because that's a condition of the permit, but she might just take fright (or *he* might become aggressive) at the sound of a whole pack of dogs barking in the distance. That would be the Naval Dog School and its noisy pupils.

But Pooch might just think it's a thousand ghosts of Just Nuisance returning to haunt him/her.

Just Nuisance has his grave close to where you park your car. Like Jock of the Bushveld he was immortalised in a book written about him. This Great Dane was more than just a dog. He was a Royal Navy mascot and did much to boost the morale of the sailors who came into contact with him.

Born in 1937, he met his end in a car accident on his seventh birthday. But in his short seven years he became a legend, with stories still being told about him today.

He was officially registered as an able-bodied seaman and posted to *HMS Afrikander*. His charge sheet showed numerous misdemeanours, including going AWOL while regularly taking the train ride to Cape Town. This was ostensibly to fetch drunken sailors back from the fleshpots of Cape Town, where he even had a bed at his disposal in the Union Jack Club.

Like any good sailor, he regularly used to get into fights with mascots from visiting ships. His fame spread so widely that he appeared in numerous publications including *Reader's Digest* and *Time* magazine. So give Just Nuisance a thought when you start this walk.

To get there, take the Redhill Road from just before Simon's Town to a lookout spot 3,5 km up the hill. It's well worth a stop to enjoy the spectacular view of Simon's Town and the naval dockyard.

From the lookout spot, continue a further 1,3 km until you come to a sign indicating the grave of Just Nuisance. Park your car here under the shade of the trees and walk a further 100 metres along Redhill Road to the start of the walk.

Three or four minutes after starting on the Jeep track (closed to traffic by two boulders at the start) you will be confronted by a fork. Take the clearer and more obvious one to the right.

Stick to this rule almost all the way to the dam, when the last fork just a few metres from the dam wall is an obvious left.

There is no route around the dam. I know. I tried finding one (some survey maps show a myriad of paths that no longer exist). In the process, I had an uncomfortably close encounter with a metre-long puff adder as thick as my forearm.

Enjoy a drinks break on the shore of the dam, built in 1964 on a farm that was known as Klein Plaats. Fish eagles can be found here, if you're lucky enough. Their plaintive cry will give you goose-flesh.

This is a walk through one of the Cape Peninsula's fynbos hot spots. For anyone with a botanical bent, this is a floral paradise. You need a permit from the Simon's Town municipality. Call (021) 786-1551.

Cape Times, February 27, 1998

Muizenberg hillside

No need
to retreat

Some places just have an aura. Have you ever been into an old, deserted farmhouse, miles from anywhere, and wondered what those walls could tell you?

Generations of heartache, happiness, euphoria and tragedy. Births and deaths. Comings and goings . . . life moves on.

The mountainside above Muizenberg gives me that feeling. Look out over a beach longer than you can ever imagine walking – all the way to Gordon's Bay – and try to picture the moment, 200 years ago at this very spot, when the Battle of Muizenberg took place. The conflict was of immense significance to South African history, for it changed 150 years of Dutch occupation to 150 years of British domination. It's hard to imagine that this peaceful little corner of False Bay could have been the scene of such hositlity.

Picture eighteen British warships, with sails set like bulging chests, pounding the Dutch troops on the shore; the Dutch falling back and digging in at a place which consequently became known as Retreat. So what's in a name?

Names that call out from the past probably all walked this path and enjoyed the same view. Cecil John Rhodes, Sir Abe Bailey, Prince Labia, Sir Herbert Baker, the Reverend Andrew Murray to name a few. They too would have enjoyed the remarkable fynbos on this little walk.

Perhaps they wouldn't have realised that one of the flowers they were looking at (*Erica urna-viridis*), is found only on this particular mountain and nowhere else in the world. And in spring, on the downhill section of this walk a flowering shrub called *Podalyria* (ertjiebos) is in full flower and gives a spectacular display. It closely resembles a sweet pea in tree form.

Start on Boyes Drive, directly opposite the clock tower on Muizenberg Station. Crude steps go straight up the mountain opposite a break in the fence, where a path comes up from the public gardens below. Climb up the steep slope from Boyes Drive for three or four minutes before reaching a T-junction and turning left.

Ten minutes of gentle uphill climb will bring you to a fork in the path, at a flat rock slab. Keep

right and slightly up, passing some steep steps on the right three minutes further on. You are now in Bailey's Kloof. From here you can watch the Battle of Muizenberg from a grandstand seat and with a little imagination.

I've often been seen staring blankly seaward, as I relive the battle. But much more real is to look down on Bailey's Cottage, a thatched building almost in the sea. It once belonged to Sir Abe Bailey (1865-1940), a prominent mining magnate and politician around the turn of the century. His grave, on a circular podium, can be seen about 50 metres below Boyes Drive.

Continue your gentle climb until the path starts a series of zigzags back down to the road. The walk is only 1,5 km one way and will take about fifty minutes. Either stroll back along Boyes Drive (1,1 km) or have a car waiting at the end (if you decide on a one-way walk, leave a car just beyond 110 Boyes Drive).

And reflect on which way our history might have gone if the Dutch had dug in a bit deeper at what became known as Retreat.

Cape Times, March 6, 1998

Sillery Trail

Meet Boris
in the pub at the end

As you read these words, I will be walking down an English country lane in north Devon, perhaps even looking out to sea at Lundy Island in the Bristol Channel.

I've always wanted to go to Lundy Island. I can't imagine why, because it's a windswept, barren piece of rock five kilometres long by one kilometre wide and populated by puffins and hermits.

It must be some rare form of Narcissus complex that draws me there. Lundy Island probably shares one thing in common with Table Mountain. Locals say it's an excellent weather vane. If you can see it, it's going to rain within 24 hours. If you can't see it, it *is* raining. It's the same with Mother Mountain.

Wish me luck that it isn't raining, because an English country lane isn't quite the same when it's belting down. With a bit of luck, there'll be a quintessentially quaint pub at the end of the lane, with lots of Dickensian characters punctuating their statements with sounds like "Ahrrrr" and "Oiiiii". But you don't need to go to all that bother. There is just such a place in Cape Town.

The walk bit is ten minutes and the drinks bit an hour or more. The Sillery Trail is one of those dozen or so Constantia urban trails which weaves its way along green belts between upmarket homes, without being intrusive. This one starts on Constantia Main Road halfway between Christ Church and the Groot Constantia turnoff, next to the Spaanschemat River.

At the beginning there is a board, as with all the Constantia urban trails, which marks the beginning of the Sillery Trail. That was until some mindless vandals broke it off. See the empty uprights as a damning indictment of that part of our human race which seeks only to destroy the constructive work of others.

Despite the start it's a gentle stroll across a meadow and down an English country lane, with the pleasant and unmistakable smell of horse pooh to complete the picture.

What more appropriate ending could there be to this shady stroll than a tavern with an atmosphere that will make you stay longer than you should? And the characters that go "Ahrrrr"? There's one in particular at the charming Peddlars

on the Bend tavern, marking the end of your ten-minute trail. His name is Boris. He's fat. And he's regular. He arrives promptly every day at opening time and leaves after lunch. And he becomes quite aggressive if you arrive with your dog. Which figures. He's a bull mastiff. Boris doesn't even belong to the tavern, but lives in the neighbourhood and slips down to the local when his owners are at work.

If only they knew why he was so fat. To watering hole you can add peanuts hole, chips hole and droë-wors hole.

When I asked if I could meet Boris, the manager of Peddlars, Anton Louw, said: "Sure, we'll phone him up." *Phone a dog?* Well . . . Boris is definitely not your average *Canis domesticus*.

Go and meet him. Get a good ten minutes of exercise in and then blow it all at the delightful Peddlars on the Bend. I hope *my* English country lane is as nice as yours.

Cape Times, March 13, 1998

Cecilia Forest

Not named
after a lady

This week's conundrum: if you take a man's family name and add "ia", it becomes a country. Take the same man's first name and add "ia" and it becomes a forest. Who is he?

It's tempting to print the answer upside down on the back page, but the sports editor won't allow it. He says he doesn't see any connection between rugby, soccer and cricket and an upside-down Cecil John Rhodes.

Cecilia Forest was named not after a Victorian maiden, but after the man who owned it. The empire builder himself.

Heaven knows why the apparently feminine form of his name was used, but it is unlikely to have anything to do with the fact that he spoke in a high-pitched, almost effeminate voice. Or that a business opponent in the Kimberley Club once called him a "limp-wristed ponce".

Harsh words indeed for a man who achieved way beyond the wildest dreams of even the most ambitious of men.

His spectacular successes in business and politics are legendary. Not to mention his education. Who in the world hasn't heard of a Rhodes Scholarship?

The land on which the University of Cape Town stands was a gift to the nation from him. The UCT post office is known as "Rhodes Gift" and all mail posted there is franked as such. It even has its own postal code.

Even more amazing is that his incredible wealth and political successes (he was prime minister of the Cape Colony, apart from being filthy, dirty rich) were achieved in a relatively short lifetime before he died at the age of 48.

But enough of him. What about his apparently feminine forest?

Well, it's just been cut down. Or at least a large part of it has. It was a fairly bland walk until the eighty-year-old pines were felled a few months ago, now revealing splendid views across the Cape Flats.

Some of the trees were becoming diseased with age and it was decided to "harvest" (forester-speak for "cut down") the rest before they caught the dreaded illness.

But for those who like pine forests – I'm not one of them; give me fynbos any day – you'll be pleased to know they are planting

more pine trees. In the meantime enjoy the view.

The walk starts at the Cecilia Forest parking area on Rhodes Drive between Kirstenbosch and Constantia Nek. Rhodes Drive was not named *after* the man. It simply *belonged* to him. In a way, it was the driveway running through his property, which stretched from Groote Schuur Hospital to Constantia Nek.

From the parking area, follow the gravel road up for a few minutes until it does a sharp bend back on itself to the right.

At this point, don't take the bend but carry straight on along a Jeep track which runs more or less parallel to Rhodes Drive some way below.

After ten to fifteen minutes, another Jeep track will join you from the right quarter. This is your return route, but just 100 metres further on is a pleasant stream, suitable for a tea break.

Retrace your steps from the stream and return along the upper route via the forest station.

Cape Times, March 20, 1998

Constantia Nek to Kirstenbosch

Walk to breakfast

What could possibly go together as well as Stilton cheese and a good Port? I found myself reflecting on this just the other day while allowing the two to roll around together on my tongue.

I know, I said to myself – a gentle walk in the forest followed by a champagne breakfast. And you'd be surprised how easy it is.

The walk starts at Constantia Nek and the breakfast starts at the Kirstenbosch restaurant. The effort required to join the two takes a mere six kilometres and one hour and 45 minutes, mostly along the level.

If you don't want to walk all the way back on a full stomach, see that you have a car waiting for you at Kirstenbosch. It's a leisurely stroll through forest and fynbos and it's suitable for the whole family.

Start at Constantia Nek and follow the tar road at the Wynberg side of the picnic area. It will take you 200 metres to a gate, after which it becomes gravel. Follow the gravel road through the pine plantation in the general direction of Kirstenbosch.

Eventually you will run out of pines and gravel road as it trickles out into a path. Shortly after this the path does a ninety-degree left turn up some log steps to a sign-post. Follow the sign indicating "contour path" – here the vegetation changes from blue gums to fynbos, for you have crossed the border into Kirstenbosch.

Keep on the level for a few minutes, ignoring the first path coming up from Kirstenbosch just before Nursery Ravine. Follow the contour into the next ravine (Skeleton Gorge) and at a plaque announcing "Smuts' Track" turn down towards your breakfast, along a path delightfully wrapped in indigenous forest.

Kirstenbosch is a treasure trove of indigenous South African plants. More than 6 000 of them in fact, making this one of the world's most famous botanical gardens.

It was originally called Leendertsbos after Jan van Riebeeck appointed one Leendert Cornelissen to take charge of a woodcutter's station there. It kept this name until the late 1700s when the Kirsten family began farming in the area. The farm then passed through

various hands until it was bought in 1895 by Cecil John Rhodes for the princely sum of £9 000.

On his death in 1902 he left it in a trust for the people of South Africa. However, it was another eleven years before an act of parliament officially declared Kirstenbosch a national botanical garden.

One of Kirstenbosch's most well-known and delightful landmarks is a fraud – or, at best, a shaky urban legend.

Ever since childhood, Lady Ann Barnard's bath has conjured up for me an image of a beautiful, aristocratic lady bathing in this crystal pool, surrounded by verdant ferns and the sound of birdsong. It came as a rude surprise that she never even clapped eyes on this captivating pool.

It was built in 1811, nine years after she left the Colony, and is referred to more correctly as the Bird Bath, for not only was it built in the shape of a bird, it was built by Colonel Christopher Bird on the property which had been leased to him during his official term of office as deputy colonial secretary.

Cape Times, April 3, 1998

The Lion's Rump

Look down
on the Sunset Coast

If trees had feelings (and there are some who say they do), then a certain clump of trees on Signal Hill would feel uncomfortably out of place.

Which is a bit unfair really, because it's the surrounding vegetation that is more out of place than the grove of Outeniqua yellow-woods, Karoo thorn, wild peach and wild olives found growing about 100 metres from the parking area at the end of Signal Hill Road.

Clearly they have been planted there by the authorities to provide welcome shade for picnickers.

And fine specimens they are too, even if they might be somewhat confused by their surroundings.

Check them out this weekend and tickle the lion's back with a pleasant walk from Signal Hill to the *kramat* at the base of Lion's Head. It's a level 2,2 km and a 25-minute walk one way.

While walking along the spine, look down on one side to the cosmopolitan Sunset Coast of the Cape Peninsula. On the other side of the path is the Cape Town city bowl and majestic Mother Moun-tain brooding over it with grandeur.

Start at the main parking area and viewpoint at the very end of Signal Hill Road, leading from Kloof Nek. Begin from the Lion's Head/Sea Point corner of the parking area and ahead, directly in line with Lion's Head, you will see the bright green roof of the *kramat* – your destination.

It's the final resting place of Muslim leader Hassan Gaibe Sha Al Quadri. It is one of a number of *kramats* on the Cape Peninsula that stand as symbols of the Muslim culture, a culture which plays a major role in the personality of Cape Town.

Along the route you will pass a fenced property which belongs to the Boy Scouts and is used as a camp and training centre.

Just below this property are some derelict blockhouses which were part of a series of outposts making up the coastal defences of the Cape Peninsula during the Second World War.

The larger one was probably the operations room, from where they could direct the firing of the guns from the Lion Battery above the

harbour (from where the noon day gun is fired). Also under its control would have been the guns of Fort Wynyard next to the Waterfront and the Apostle Battery at Llandudno.

I was once poring over an old map – one of my eccentric fascinations, along with the Second World War naval battles – and was intrigued by what I saw on a 1904 map of the area just below the *kramat* and Kloof Nek.

It's now known as Tamboerskloof (translated to "Drummer's Ravine") and Higgovale, but was marked then as "German Town".

The popularity of this part of Cape Town with German people is well known. Even the Cape Town German School is there.

But it clearly goes back much further than I thought.

Once you are at the end of the walk to the *kramat*, either have another car waiting for you or return the same way.

If you enter the *Dargan (kramat)*, treat it as you would any holy place and respect the Muslim custom of removing your shoes.

Cape Times, April 17, 1998

Woodstock Cave

Great view,
pity about the graffiti

Have you ever found yourself being visually drawn back to a place? Once you know where Woodstock Cave is, you won't be able to help yourself.

Every time you see Devil's Peak, which is difficult to avoid if you work in or near the city, you will find your eyes probing the lower slopes looking for the telltale black slit which is Woodstock Cave.

Not so much a cave as a large and deep overhang, some 50 metres wide by fifteen metres deep and three or four metres high at the entrance.

In winter a waterfall forms a curtain over the centre section of the opening. The panoramic view of Table Bay and the City Bowl from inside the cave is well worth a picture.

The walk is a short series of zigzags along a path which is rough underfoot, so be sure to wear appropriate boots. High heels or flip-flops would be hopelessly out of place.

If you think that's a throwaway line, think again. I never fail to be amazed by what people wear on the mountain – including flip-flops and high heels.

Such people usually stop you and ask "where does this path go to?" I have to fight the urge to tell them not to end a sentence with a preposition, among other things. They also have no water, no rain gear and no idea. There should be a law to prevent such people having access to the mountain.

The mountain is a bit like the sea. If you don't give it the utmost respect, it will take you.

To get to the start of the walk, drive exactly five kilometres past the lower cable station along Tafelberg Road, to the end of the tarred section. A further 100 metres on dirt will get you to a metal gate with stone pillars.

The start of the climb is well hidden, just ten paces before the gate. The yellow-brown rocky face hides the beginning of the path.

The route zigzags its way slowly up the slope. After four zigzags, the path eventually reaches a contour path which circles the mountain all the way from Constantia Nek to Kloof Nek.

Cross over this important thoroughfare and start counting

the zigzags again. Do not add to the already serious erosion problem by taking short cuts. After the seventh zigzag from the contour path you will be confronted with steep log steps and rock scramble.

About ten metres before reaching this steep section, take a side path cutting back in the direction from which you have just come.

You should now be more or less level with the cave. A few minutes' walk will bring you to its mouth.

Retrace your steps to return.

One of those little disappointments in the human race that faces one on an almost daily basis will confront you on arrival at the cave.

As the world gets smaller, with more and more people cramming into less and less space, I become cynical and wonder if AIDS is perhaps not a punishment for our thoughtlessness towards each other.

Mindless fools have seen fit to carry pots of paint up here to leave their names, without any apparent shame, for all to see and despise. What is it that inspires the sick graffiti brigade to deface our natural heritage in this manner?

I would like to think that they are low-class people without culture or pride, but alas I suspect this may not be so.

Maybe they are just ordinary people who need help from a psychiatrist.

Cape Times, April 24, 1998

The Old Mule Track

Way above "Aitch-Que"

In the halcyon days of yesteryear, when Britannia ruled the waves, Simon's Town was nothing less than the headquarters of the Royal Navy for the entire southern hemisphere.

Being of North Country stock meself, I have this fascination with the utter arrogance of which the English are so capable, simply by *not* saying something.

I mean they don't say the *British* Royal Navy. Just THE Royal Navy. There's only one Royal Navy, m' boy!

Any other monarch's navy is required to be more specific.

Just as we have the South African Rugby Football Union, the Welsh RFU, the French RFU and Uncle Tom Cobley 'n all's RFU, there is only one that is called *The* Rugby Football Union. And everyone knows it is based at "Aitch-Que" in Twickenham.

Chances are if you addressed a letter to the *English* Rugby Football Union, it would be studiously ignored.

But don't ignore the blockhouses to which the Old Mule Track above Simon's Town leads. They are very basic and down-to-earth. In fact, there's an air of mystery about them.

They are thought to be relics of the Anglo-Boer War, but no one seems to be quite sure, including the Simon's Town Museum.

The return walk to the two blockhouses will take $2^1/_2$ hours, treating you to superb views over False Bay, blackbearded proteas and orange-breasted sunbirds.

There is no water or shade, so this one is for now, when the winter flowering blackbearded protea is starting to flaunt its beauty.

You will also see an alien plant invader, the Port Jackson willow, which is being brought under control by a fungus. Evidence of this is clearly visible on the first part of this walk. *Uromycladium tepperianum* is one hell of a name to handle, but it sure is effective when it comes to wiping out the invasive Port Jackson.

Notice what a friend of mine rather coarsely refers to as "flying elephant turds" hanging from the branches. This brown rust fungus, imported from Australia to do the hatchet job, causes the cells of the host tree to multiply and enlarge in a "cancerous" type of growth, and

also taps the vascular system.

Rather like an arboreal vampire, it sucks the tree to death. And good riddance, I say.

To get to the start of the walk, drive through Simon's Town until you come to the police station on the far side of town.

Then travel exactly one kilometre beyond the police station. This will bring you to the Simon's Town school. Turn right after the school up Harington Road and then to the end of Jan Smuts Drive where you will find a track going straight up the mountain.

Walk straight up the stone asphalt track for 150 metres until it forks. Take the right-hand fork on to gravel. A further 200 metres along this eroded gravel track it becomes tar and stone again – but only on the corner.

On this tarred corner, leave the track and follow the path which marks the upper level of a firebreak, towards Simon's Town.

After about five minutes along the firebreak path it seems to run out at a point opposite the middle of the school, and above some tennis courts.

At this point look for a rocky cairn on the left of the path.

This marks the beginning of the Old Mule Track and you're on your way to a fascinating view of history and nature at work.

Cape Times, May 15, 1998

Newlands Forest to Rhodes Memorial

All-year-round walk

Try to imagine a statue on the very top of Lion's Head, fully the height and size of a fifty-storey building. Oh Lordy! The very thought is perfectly revolting. As if the twenty-something-storey pepperpots on the side of Devil's Peak weren't bad enough. But fifty storeys on top would have been just too much.

As unlikely as it may seem today, a serious proposal was made after the death of Cecil John Rhodes in 1902 to erect a 500-foot-high statue in honour of the man. After much debate, the present memorial was opted for and officially opened on Rhodes's birthday on 5 July 1912 – some ten years after his death. It occupies the site of one of his favourite viewpoints.

Even Rhodes, the empire builder, would surely have cringed at the thought of himself magnified a hundred times standing on top of Lion's Head for eternity. It would have added a whole new meaning to the Colossus of Rhodes. And probably would have made him turn in his Matopos.

What finished up being Rhodes Memorial, at which this walk ends, was designed by Sir Herbert Baker and funded by public contributions. But Rhodes's real memorial is perhaps the University of Cape Town, for he donated the land on which it stands today.

Start the walk at Newlands Forest (after having left a car at Rhodes Memorial) and follow the signs to the contour path. Surprisingly it will take a steady 45 to 55 minutes to climb from Union Avenue to the contour path.

One doesn't imagine Newlands Forest to be that big – but it is.

This is a pleasant walk for any time of the year, as it is almost entirely in shade. Once at the contour path (which stretches from Constantia Nek to Kloof Nek), turn right.

For the next hour stroll along the level, in and out of ravines and under the canopy of dense forest. Stuff that will make you feel good to be alive.

Along the way you will come first to one stile and then another. Turn down at the second stile and descend to your waiting car.

The land between the stiles is Rhodes Estate. Don't forget that this incredible man not only owned

and lived in Groote Schuur, but owned virtually all of the land from here to Constantia Nek.

But that's not all. He planned to have the map of Africa coloured red in an unbroken strip from Cape to Cairo. If it weren't for a few "pesky Frogs" getting in the way, he could just have done it.

One cannot help being amazed at the awesome power accumulated by a sickly man who died of ill health at the tender age of 48.

The debate about whether he was gay or not will rage on, far into the future. Who cares? He was a remarkable man, despite a colleague in the Kimberley Club calling him a "limp-wristed ponce".

He was Prime Minister of the Cape Colony, controller of both De Beers diamond mines in Kimberley and the Goldfields Company on the Reef, as well as having a long list of other offices and functions. It seems he held every senior position in government and commerce. Short of being the local scoutmaster, that is. Which was probably just as well.

At the end of your two-and-a-half-hour walk, reflect on this legend of a man over a good English cuppa at the tearoom.

Cape Times, May 22, 1998

The Baboon shipwrecks

The gulls
cash in

Who says lightning never strikes in the same place twice? Ships seem to make a habit of striking the same rock twice, so why not lightning?

There must be hundreds of places around the world where the remains of two ships sit almost one on top of the other. You'd have thought the icon on the chart denoting "wreck" would be enough to make any self-respecting officer-of-the-watch steer well clear.

But apparently not. Some rocks seem to be huge magnets. Just such a place is the focal point of an interesting coastal walk in the Cape of Good Hope Nature Reserve.

Hoek van Bobbejaan (Baboon's Corner) is the strange name of a place to which ships are fatally attracted. Perhaps the baboons were on the ships. Anyway, it makes a nice walk of just under two hours.

Don't be alarmed by the notice at the beginning of the walk which describes it as a three-hour circular route.

The only way it could take three hours is on your hands and knees. And that way you don't get to see much. So remain upright and enjoy the outward journey along the coast and the return trip along the clifftops of Kommetjieberg.

At the point you are headed for are two shipwrecks, although only one is visible. The *Aggre* (1961) had probably disintegrated by the time the *Phylissia* (1968) came to sit on top of her. The *Phylissia* was a 450-ton I & J trawler that ran aground just before midnight on 2 May 1968. Her crew was rescued by helicopter with, thankfully, no casualties.

The only beneficiaries of her thirty-ton cargo of fish were the resident gulls. Probably looking down their noses at such scavenging would have been the African black oystercatchers, with their distinctive bright red legs, bill and eyes. They are said to be the most endangered of our sea birds, but you will almost certainly see them along this stretch of coast.

To get to the start, enter the Cape of Good Hope Nature Reserve after paying a modest fee at the gate. Then drive about 4,4 km into the reserve before coming to a turnoff to the right marked "Circular Drive". Ignore this and take the next turnoff – also marked

"Circular Drive".

Follow the signs to Gifkommetjie where there is a parking area and the start of the walk.

You will see on the walk, apart from the rare oystercatchers, an abundance of tortoises and rock lizards.

On your return, with the aid of binoculars, you will no doubt see buck on the open plains, visible from the height of the ridge.

Follow the coast north for about two kilometres until you reach a rocky peninsula – the Hoek van Bobbejaan – the final resting place of the *Aggre* and the *Phylissia*. The area is covered in buck droppings, so it is obviously a favourite spot for them.

Don't go beyond the shipwreck as you would be trespassing on a private beach. The vast area of private land to the north, along with a scattering of buildings and a long white beach, used to be a part of a much larger property belonging to the Hare family. The family tried to start its own private nature reserve but its noble efforts were denied by poachers.

As a result, the family presented the farm to the authorities as the nucleus of a wildlife reserve on condition that it could retain its seaside cottage at Brightwater, along with the surrounding area, for its own use.

This fine gesture was one of the factors resulting in the formation of the Cape of Good Hope Nature Reserve in July 1939.

Cape Times, May 29, 1998

Elsie's Peak

Have a
whale of a time

"Climb a mountain to see whales?" a hiking mate asked disbelievingly. "Are you on drugs or what?" Well, no. I mean, *no*, most definitely *not*. Unless my asthma pump dispenses hallucinogens of which I am unaware.

But you don't need drugs to see whales from the top of Elsie's Peak, between Fish Hoek and Glencairn.

Just binoculars.

Between August and October you will see enough southern right whales to die for, doll. Talking of which – rather sadly – they are called "right" whales because they were the right whales to kill.

They float when they're dead and there's nothing more inconvenient for whale hunters than a sinking dead whale. Jolly sporting of the whales, I say.

The view from Elsie's Peak is most rewarding. Glencairn and Simon's Town – with its flock of bobbing small craft – lie just below.

On the other side Fish Hoek, Kalk Bay and Muizenberg lie at the beginning of a majestic sweep all the way around False Bay to Hangklip.

The way to the top is easy. Either choose the linear return route from the Fish Hoek side, starting from Ravine Steps. Or go for the easier circular route up from the Glencairn side. Either way in springtime you will be guaranteed to see whales. If you are particularly lucky and the whales are frisky, you will be treated to a breach or two.

When a whale breaches it leaps almost clear of the water and comes crashing down on its side. Awesome. It's an absolute mindblow when you look at the southern right whale's vital statistics. Eighteen metres long and weighing 45 tons – the weight of ten elephants! Imagine this enormous mammal coming straight out of the water, the height of a six-storey building from nose to tail, and then tilting to one side to plummet back. The effect is awesome.

So who needs drugs?

As large as our southern right whales may seem, they are nowhere near the size of the largest animal that ever lived on this planet. A dinosaur, I hear you say. No. The 140-ton, thirty-metres blue whales – which at this very moment are frolicking around the Antarctic –

are three times the weight of any dinosaur that ever existed. Not to mention thirty elephants.

While contemplating the frolicking whales from the top of Elsie's Peak, you might be wondering who the heck Elsie was anyway.

I asked lots of people in Fish Hoek where Elsie fitted into their local history and finally struck gold at the Fish Hoek library.

It seems she was never anybody. She was a tree. And that probably applies to all the other Elsie's Rivers and Elsie's Peaks around the country.

This particular peak takes its name from the river which flows below it through the Glencairn Valley – the Elsiesrivier. The river in turn took its name from the "elsje" or "rooiels" trees which used to line its banks.

Not only was the name corrupted to Elsie, but the rooiels trees were displaced by alien plant invaders. The rooiels is also known by its English names of red alder or butterspoon tree. The latter name arises from the shape of the growing tip at the apex of each branch.

Cape Times, June 5, 1998

Klaassensbosch

A microcosm of
our indigenous trees

For a couple of my hiking books I developed a simple grading system to give the reader a reasonably accurate picture of what to expect. It makes allowance for people who suffer from a fear of heights – and there seem to be a surprisingly large number of them.

I measured the effort needed to complete the walk on a scale of one to four and combined it with a fear of heights (if the potential exists) on a scale of A to D.

Thus a 1A hike is an easy stroll with no exposure to heights and a 4D is really scary if you have a heights problem and is only for the very fit.

It worked just fine, until I met my wonderful wife. She taught me a much easier grading system. And it's one our friends swear by, thanks to its incredible accuracy.

Now all hikes are either a one whinge hike or a five whinge hike, or something in-between. You don't even want to think about a seven or eight whinge hike. That's more of a high-pitched plaintive cry than your actual under-the-breath whinge.

Today's walk is a zero whinge hike. Klaassensbosch could even be tackled by your ageing grandmother.

I had always imagined Kirstenbosch National Botanical Garden to be entirely above Rhodes Drive. So it came as a surprise to learn that a small part of it is actually below the road – between the Rycroft Gate (or so-called "Top Gate") of Kirstenbosch and the parking area of Cecilia Forest.

The area is known as Klaassensbosch and is a microcosm of our indigenous trees. A broad Jeep track stretches from the start in Hohenort Avenue to Top Gate; a distance of a mere 500 metres. But in that short stretch you will see silver trees, yellowwoods, wild peach, wild olive, mountain cypress, keurboom, rooiels and many others.

Van Riebeeck's hedge is very close by and some of the offspring from its indigenous wild almond trees can be seen. It was planted to demarcate the boundaries of the colony and prevent the Khoi from nicking the cattle and sheep.

The burghers had increasingly been encroaching on the herding ground of the Khoi and in retaliation the indigenous herders helped

themselves to the cattle. Which seemed fair enough at the time.

The wild almond has many thick, tangled trunks and when brambles were planted between them, it made entry difficult and the removal of cattle impossible.

Another interesting member of the arboreal population is the Cape beech. I'd be interested to know if any reader can tell me the origin of its Dutch/Afrikaans name of *boekenhout* (books wood). Whether they made paper from it I don't know, but they certainly made violins. The wood was highly prized for its fine grain and durability –

essential qualities for a squawk box.

This little-known corner of Kirstenbosch was not always as pristine as it is today. From the early 1900s until as recently as 1978 this land was completely overrun by alien gums, pines and blackwoods, planted there for commercial purposes.

In the 1980s Kirstenbosch became involved in a major regeneration process and gradually removed most of the aliens. Slowly but surely the natural fauna and birdlife are beginning to re-establish themselves.

Cape Times, June 12, 1998

The Yellowwood Trail, Kirstenbosch

And snobbish silver trees

Yellowwood is highly sought after for making high-quality furniture. But it is certainly not the only tree you will see on the Yellowwood Trail. With the help of nameplates you will be able to identify many other indigenous trees, including Cape beech, Cape chestnut, Cape saffron, ironwood, stinkwood, and wild peach.

This is one of the three clearly marked trails laid out in the vast grounds of Kirstenbosch National Botanical Gardens. This one winds its way up the densely wooded slopes to the contour path and then down again through more indigenous forest.

Almost the entire walk is in shade and is therefore ideal for either summer or winter walking. None of the indigenous trees is deciduous (lose their leaves in winter), so you are assured of a dense canopy all year round. As easy walks go, this one is moderately strenuous, as there are very few level sections. It is either up or down, but nowhere is it excessively steep.

Start at the turnstiles, where you will be required to pay an entrance fee.

Once inside, continue straight through the covered alleyway past the information bureau past the lecture hall and down some steps. Follow the sign pointing to the Smuts Track and Yellowwood Trail.

Now you are on your way and need only to follow the well-placed signboards for the next hour and a half. It is a 3,2-km circular route through beautiful natural forest.

Near the end of the trail, you will come to a section marked by many healthy looking silver tree saplings. These are very special for greater Cape Town, for they grow naturally nowhere else in the world.

Even within this area, they are somewhat snobbish about their address. Reasonably sized stands are confined to only three places: Kirstenbosch, the Helderberg Basin around Somerset West and the southern slopes of Lion's Head.

Numerous attempts have been made to cultivate them elsewhere in the world, but they seem to represent your typical Capetonians – they want to live here and nowhere else.

Nothing can quite compare with the shimmering and glinting of the

leaves in a gentle breeze. The silver hairy covering of the leaves protects them from dehydration during summer.

But there is a downside to these arboreal kings of the Cape. They are very susceptible to root and collar rot caused by a fungus. This explains the common sight of an occasional dead tree among a group of healthy ones. The mortality rate is particularly high at the seedling stage.

But, at the end of your walk you can have a delightful champagne breakfast (or just a beer) at the restaurant close to the entrance. That should prevent any root rot and make you feel that the whole exercise was worthwhile.

Cape Times, July 3, 1998

Muizenberg Cave

With some
flower power

Where else in the world can you get on a train, travel a relatively short distance (in this case to Muizenberg) and get off at a station where the sea and beautiful beach stretch far into the distance from one platform – and towering above the other platform is a mountain which takes a little more than an hour to climb? Just to add to all this, history surrounds you, and the views, plant and bird life en route are magnificent.

Why not take the train to Muizenberg this weekend and do a circular trip around the mountain above Muizenberg Station? As a bonus, you'll get a cave which goes all of fifty metres right through the mountain.

Allow three hours from start to finish and remember to take a torch. From the station, walk up through the public park opposite and come out onto Boyes Drive. Almost opposite, but slightly to the right, are some crude steps going straight up the mountain. Take them and after three minutes of up-hill slog, turn left at a T-junction. Within ten to fifteen minutes you will be on your way up Bailey's

Kloof, with splendid views across the whole of False Bay. Below is the spot where the Battle of Muizenberg took place nearly two centuries ago.

Flowering on the mountain in spring is an extremely rare erica called *Erica urna-viridis* (meaning erica resembling a green urn). It's a very pretty, almost greenish-white erica, sticky to the touch. What is so special about it, is that it occurs only on this mountain above Muizenberg and *nowhere else in the world*.

At the top of the kloof the path leads into Mimetes Valley, a breatktakingly beautiful sight between June and November, when the mimetes tree is in full red flower power.

After half an hour of easy walking along Mimetes Valley, the path spills onto a gravel road, which immediately presents you with three possibilities. Take the right-hand fork up and after 200 metres keep a sharp eye open for a path off the gravel road, to the right. This will take you within five minutes to Muizenberg Cave at the top of the ridge.

Explore the cave, but be careful

of slippery rocks at the begining. Soon you will find you need to go on hands and knees on a sandy floor, in order to crawl through the last forty metres to emerge on the southern side of the ridge.

On returning to the gravel road, turn right and follow it up and over the hill and down to Junction Pool.

Turn right at the T-junction and follow the gravel road until it passes between tall radio masts, eventually wasting into a clear path descending down Farmer Peck's Valley, named after the innkeeper brothers Peck.

Cape Times, January 15, 1994

Lion's Head

Was there once gold in that thar hill?

Where is the southernmost gold mine in Africa? Somewhere in the Free State? Try Lion's Head.

As unlikely as it now seems, a company known as the Lion's Head Gold Mining Syndicate was formed in 1887 following so-called expert advice. They sank a shaft some thirty metres deep – so this was no mere arbitrary scratching of the surface. Some gold quartz was said to have been found, and in no time at all Lion's Head was teeming with prospective million-aires.

Needless to say, the gold rush soon fizzled out when tests showed the quantities to be uneconomical. Just imagine, though, if it had been viable. With beautiful scenery, wine, oil *and* gold, we Kaapenaars would have been even more smug and self-satisfied than we already appear to be. In fact, we could have become unbearable. Just look what it's done to others from the North. Ah well. At least we can use the sour grapes to make distilling wine.

The remnants of the mine are still there, about 100 metres below the tar road at the beginning of this walk. This is probably the best value-for-energy hike in the Cape Peninsula. For the minimum of effort you are treated to a kaleido-scope of views as you spiral your way to the top.

The start is near Kloof Nek along the Signal Hill Road. The gravel track leading off the tar road rises gently through a most impressive stand of silver trees (*Leucadendron argenteum*). This unique tree is at its most beautiful in a gentle breeze with leaves glinting in the sunlight.

After fifteen minutes the track narrows to a wide path and you enjoy a wide range of views as you spiral around the mountain. After almost one revolution, you will come to a large pine tree in the path and some 200 metres on, a second pine, beyond which you will see a set of chains that help you to climb the rock face. Don't be put off by the chains. The way up is not difficult, even if you do have a fear of heights. The chains are really cosmetic; rather like a Linus blanket for those who need reassuring. If, however, you have a serious fear of heights, you can in fact take a longer route which avoids the chains altogether. (Take

the steps which leave the main path about thirty metres before the first pine.)

But assuming you take the "brave" route, scramble up the first eight-metre chain, then immediately up another shorter one. Now climb the slope directly above to another rock face where a third and fourth chain will help you. Then follow the four pines diagonally up to the left. At the last pine double back up the ridge, using a three-metre ladder. From the ladder, it looks like heavy going, but it's only another ten minutes to the top. And when you get there – what a panorama!

At night under a full moon this climb is sheer magic. Why not try it around sunset and get the best of both worlds?

Cape Times, February 12, 1994

Constantia Nek to Chapman's Peak Drive

Plant persuaded to produce wasps

For a long sobering lesson on the botanical sins of our forefathers, take a walk this weekend from Constantia Nek to Hout Bay – over the top. The top is interesting in itself, for Vlakkenberg (or Flags Mountain) was an important link in the communication chain of the early Dutch settlers.

Leave your car at Constantia Nek (remembering to arrange return transport from Hout Bay) and walk down the road about 150 metres towards Hout Bay. When you reach a sign indicating a footpath to Vlakkenberg, go through a gap in the fence. Then follow the road around a reservoir to the top left-hand corner of the fenced-off area. Again go through a gate in the fence and follow it for 75 metres, after which the path veers away to the right and begins climbing the slope.

At this point you might have noticed an appalling infestation of wattle. Higher up, it's wall-to-wall hakea and further still, blue gums. All three are highly unwelcome invaders from Australia, threatening to choke our indigenous fynbos.

The fruits of the richest floral kingdom in the world are nowhere to be seen. But all is not lost . . . Look carefully at the long-leafed wattle and you will see what appear to be large green or brown berries. These are the results of a wasp (imported from Australia, like the wattle itself) that rather cheekily lays its eggs in the ovary of the flower. The flower aborts and produces a wart-like growth around the invaders. If you were to take a penknife and carefully cut one of these in half, you would find two or three wriggling grubs inside, but only if the "berry" or gall is green.

If it is brown, you will see tiny holes where the juvenile wasps bored their way out, to repeat the cycle. *These plants will never again produce seeds — only wasps.* This type of biological control is the only hope of saving our beautiful fynbos from eradication by aliens.

It's a relief to leave the blue gums behind and start climbing the steep slope of Vlakkenberg Nek surrounded by a wide variety of everlastings, ericas, crassula and protea.

When the white beacon on top of Vlakkenberg draws level with your right shoulder, continue on the path for another fifty metres and look for the faint path leading to it. It is well worth the five-minute detour. The view of the Hout Bay valley far below is breathtaking. In the eighteenth century, if a foreign man o' war was sighted off Hout Bay, a horseman would ride up to Vlakkenberg where flags would alert the people of Wynberg, who would repeat the signal to Newlands and then on to the Castle in Cape Town.

Return to the main path, which soon descends and crosses a stream, before climbing up again and suddenly bursting out on to a tar road. Two minutes on this road and you rejoin a path heading south. Soon the Sentinel guarding Hout Bay harbour comes into sight.

Follow the straight and narrow for another 45 minutes along a more or less level contour, until it drops rapidly into Chapman's Peak Drive via a gravel forestry road, ending at a parking area 200 metres beyond East Fort.

Cape Times, February 26, 1994

The manganese mine of Hout Bay

Victim of a poor transport system

The Cape Peninsula seems to be peppered with mines that somehow never got off the ground, so to speak: the tin mine on Devil's Peak, Steenberg's silver mine and the failed gold mine on Lion's Head.

Add to those Hout Bay's manganese mine, where you can still handle the low-grade manganese ore, abandoned in huge piles outside some of its eight shafts.

Even take a piece home if you want – no one will miss it from the estimated 3 000 tons still waiting in vain to be shipped after 85 years! The walk is an easy one, and should only take two to three hours, depending on how many shafts you want to look down.

But then if you've seen one black hole, you've seen them all, so two hours should be enough. The longest shaft (No. 4) goes all of 84 metres horizontally into the mountain.

Start from just beyond East Fort on Chapman's Peak Drive, where the gravel forestry road cuts back towards Hout Bay. Walk up this gravel road to the point where it doubles back on itself.

About 150 metres after the hairpin bend, keep a sharp eye open for a path which leaves the gravel road and is marked by a rocky cairn. This path soon zigzags its way up the slope. Count the zigzags and just after the fourth bend the path forks. Keep to the left level path and it will lead you under an old fence directly to No. 7 shaft. The really long one (No. 4 shaft) is higher up the slope directly above.

After numerous attempts, 1909 seems to be the first year in which manganese was successfully mined and shipped out of Hout Bay. The first customer was a company in Belgium. As manganese occurs fairly high up on the mountainside, it was necessary to devise some economical means of transporting it down to the waiting ship.

The remains of the jetty can still be clearly seen. To get the ore down to the jetty, the miners erected a crude corrugated iron chute which proved to be not all that effective.

At 750 metres in length down a steep 30° gradient, the ore tended to run out of control and fly off in all the wrong directions. Some of the old rusted iron sheets can still be seen. A combination of the failed transport problem coupled with an

ever-decreasing quality of ore, led to the closure of the mine after only two years, in 1911.

An urban legend – popular in Hout Bay – that the first load of ore went down the chute and straight through the bottom of a waiting ship, while colourful and even amusing, is simply not true. An examination of the angle and construction of the jetty will show the story up to be what it is – a myth. Early photographs in the local museum show the ore being transported along the jetty in coco-pans. Quite apart from which there is simply no wreck to substantiate the tale.

The manganese content of the ore varied widely and in some cases the ore was more iron than manganese. The largest tunnel had ore assaying at iron 43% and man-ganese nil. Some manganese mine!

Cape Times, March 12, 1994

The Peninsula Trail

See the
waterworks museum

It was a dream of the late John Wiley, when he was Minister of Environmental Affairs, to establish a hiking trail from Cape Town to Cape Point. The idea was eventually dropped, as it was felt the overnight huts would be too close to civilisation and therefore prone to being vandalised. There is a paradox there somewhere.

Despite the rather sad indictment of our society, you can do your own Peninsula trail if you're prepared to spend a few hard-earned shekels on your overnight stop. The beauty of this incredible Peninsula of ours is that you can walk 38 km down its backbone and cross a tar road only twice between Kloof Nek and Kalk Bay.

This is a two-day hike with an overnight stop at luxury holiday bungalows just below Constantia Nek. A big plus for this trail, apart from the obviously splendid views and rich fynbos, is a great lunch stop and end to each of the two days. Day one starts at Kloof Nek with lunch in the aptly named Valley of Isolation, finishing the day's seven-hour/eighteen-kilometre walk at Houtkappers-

poort (call 794-5216) or Silvermist (call 794-7601). Supper can either be in your self-catering luxury bungalow or 100 metres up the road at the rustic Constantia Nek restaurant.

Just after your lunch stop on day one, and before walking on the high wall of Woodhead Reservoir, don't miss the little known Waterworks Museum, established in 1973 by a retired member of the Cape Town City Council engineering staff, Terence Timoney. It is absolutely fascinating, even for non-museum freaks.

The walls are adorned with well-preserved pictures of the building of the Table Mountain reservoirs more than a century ago. And apart from various artefacts there is even a full-on steam engine which was used to haul the heavy equipment from the old cableway at the top of Kasteels Poort to the dam site. As we had not yet discovered coal in South Africa (now a major export), they had to import coal all the way from Wales and lug it up the old cableway to power this iron horse. Arrange to get the key from the nearby overseer's house or phone

Terence Timoney on (021) 689-2288.

Day two starts with a climb but soon levels out to a more or less even path for the rest of the day (eight hours/twenty kilometres).

Lunch could be turned into a grand affair in the tranquil setting of Silvermine Reservoir. All you have to do is persuade a good friend to meet you there with cold Castles and glowing braai coals.

From the Silvermine reservoir the route follows the river course until it crosses the tar road at the top of Ou Kaapseweg, thence past the Kalk Bay caves and down Echo Valley, finally ending at Kalk Bay railway station.

While waiting for a train to take you back to Cape Town you might like to pop in to the conveniently placed and convivial Brass Bell restaurant right on the station and overlooking the sea. But beware: the atmosphere is so congenial in the pub that our party was forced to miss four trains in a row!

Cape Times, April 9, 1994

Cecilia waterfall

A thousand
harp strings

Cecilia Forest is a very popular spot for a Sunday stroll with the family dog under the shade of elderly pine trees. But with just a bit more effort, you could work up a good sweat, enjoy some wonderful views and be back at your car in under two hours. Cecilia waterfall, some way above the canopy of the forest, is at its best in summer when it is a gentle waterfall of a thousand harp strings tautly strung between verdant moss and ferns.

This walk starts from Rhodes Drive, opposite the turn-off to the Cellars Hohenort Country House Hotel. Leave your car at the entrance to Cecilia Forest and climb over the wooden fence where it ends at the Main Road, and follow the wire fence in the direction of Kirstenbosch until you cross a stream 100 metres further on. Follow the stream upwards for ten minutes, crossing first one gravel road, then arriving at another, where you turn right, following the road until it becomes a path.

Notice the pine trees are of a particular type – straight up and down main trunks with small branches coming out at regular intervals in radial groupings. These are commercially viable because all the knots appear at regular intervals where the branches radiate out from one point on the trunk. Also the main trunk is straight, unlike the pines commonly found in suburbia such as the stone pine and cluster pine.

The path will lead you up some log steps before coming to a comprehensive sign at the boundary to Kirstenbosch Botanical Gardens. Just ten metres beyond the sign turn sharp left up some more log steps marked "Cecilia Ravine". This is where you will work up a good sweat, but the unfolding vista makes it all worthwhile.

The climb takes you first into one wooded ravine and then into a second bigger one, thick with indigenous forest. This is where you will find the pretty Cecilia waterfall. It's a lovely spot, full of peace and tranquillity . . . a perfect place for morning tea.

Once you have refreshed your body and soul, climb out of Cecilia Ravine and you will soon see your zigzag route down Spilhaus Ravine.

About fifteen minutes of gentle

descent will bring you to some concrete settling tanks. Don't follow the Jeep track you now see, but rather follow the river course the rest of the way back to your car. The area of the concrete tanks is known officially as the "Old Picnic Site", but a regular climbing friend of mine prefers to call it "Bacon & Eggs Corner", as we have detected that gorgeous aroma from 100 metres up!

Cape Times, April 16, 1994

The Sentinel circuit

The French flirtation

Who would have thought that the French occupied the Cape? Well they did – for all of $2^1/_2$ years, and their headquarters were in no more unlikely a place than Hout Bay.

Take a walk around the Sentinel this weekend, and you will stumble across five large cannon at the beginning and end of the circuit. They form part of the West Fort. (The French also built East Fort on the opposite side of the bay, on Chapman's Peak Drive.)

In 1781, the French support of the American War of Independence against the British was recognised by the Netherlands. This immediately put the Cape in jeopardy of attack by the British, and it wasn't long before Britain did just that – choosing Hout Bay as the soft underbelly.

To their immense surprise however, the French, now in alliance with the Dutch, anticipated the move (through a spy in Plymouth) and landed first, to help lay down a battery of "20 pieces of cannon" at this very spot, thus starting the $2^1/_2$-year French military occupation of the Cape in support of the Dutch colonists. Any enemy of the English was a friend of France.

This interesting walk begins and ends at the parking area next to West Fort, beyond the last entrance to Hout Bay Harbour. Allow a good two hours for the circuit, which includes some rock hopping – so be sure to have suitable footwear. Also take plenty of liquid refreshment as there is water, water everywhere, but not a drop to drink. A final word of advice: if you have a fear of heights, stay at home. The path is clearly defined, but in places rather precipitous. It's no more difficult than walking on a pavement, except the gutter is rather a long way down.

From the gun battery, follow the coast past the new sewage plant and soon the dirt road will peter out at an old incinerator. Move on, past the ravages of civilisation and into an unspoilt world under the ominous shadow of the Sentinel towering way above you. Then pick your way across a rocky landslide, which is probably the result of the sheer face of the Sentinel having collapsed into the sea. As this probably happened thousands of years ago, don't be too concerned about a repeat performance as you

pass by. The path now hugs the steep face and descends gingerly to cross a bay of cannonball rocks. Make sure you exit this bay through a large hole between the granite boulders, and not by scaling the rocks to the right – the infinitely more difficult way.

Soon you will find yourself rounding the corner and the mysterious "other side" comes into view with the Duiker Point peninsula and, separated from it by a narrow stretch of water, Duiker Island – incorrectly billed as Seal Island by the tourist pleasure launches. Which is perfectly excusable, as the island is wall-to-wall seals with hardly a duiker in sight. The seals' territorial squabbling and barking can be heard from some distance.

The uphill slog to the nek above is only twenty minutes and the rest is an easy lope down past the fishing community flats. Once back at the cannon, don't feel too sorry about the Poms having come all that way in vain, back in 1781. After the initial shock of a French encounter, they sailed on to Saldanha Bay and set upon six Dutch East Indiamen hiding there, richly laden on their return from the East.

Cape Times, April 30, 1994

Elephant's Eye Cave

Jumbo walk
to berg cave

Like the elephant, you'll never forget the view from inside this cave, with the majestic sweep of False Bay framed by its entrance.

Elephant's Eye Cave is on the middle slopes of the Constantiaberg and, from most parts of Tokai, this section of mountainside takes on the shape of an elephant's head and trunk. The cave is in just the right position to be the elephant's eye.

There are a few routes by which to reach it, but perhaps the easiest is from the Silvermine Reservoir, giving you the advantage of climbing most of the height by car up Ou Kaapseweg.

From the far end of the Silvermine Reservoir parking area there are three routes: two gravel roads and a path between them. Take the right-hand gravel road in the direction of the Constantiaberg mast. Three minutes later you should pass a stone building (public toilet) on your left. Another six minutes will bring you to a crossroads. To the left there is a sand track and to the right, a road covered in short grass. Take the grassy route which joins up with a gravel road running parallel to the first one.

On reaching the T-junction where the grassy road meets the new gravel road, turn left. This road will wind its way up the hill ahead for ten to fifteen minutes.

At a point near the top, you will come to a place where the road surface is reinforced with a double concrete strip.

Leave the road here along a path leading off to the right. This will take you to the edge of a pine forest, which it skirts to its far end, crossing over the headwaters of the Prinzkasteel Stream.

Once over the stream, you will immediately see the Tokai Forest fire-lookout hut on the skyline directly ahead. This is your next objective, and from there you will clearly see the cave and the path to it.

Enjoy the superb sight of the rolling green vineyards of a verdant Constantia on an autumn day. Long may the developers keep their hands off them!

Return the same way and you should be back at your car (or a waiting braai alongside the Silvermine Reservoir) in about two hours

and fifteen minutes. While walking alongside the pine forest, you may notice some alien long-leafed wattle, with what appear to be shrivelled black berries (or fresh firm green ones, depending on the time of year). These "berries" are in fact galls or unnatural outgrowths caused by a fascinating little insect known as a gall wasp.

The gall wasp is systematically wiping out the invasive long-leafed wattle to the thunderous applause of conservationists and those concerned with the fate of our fynbos. This method of biological control of alien plants is enjoying spectacular success.

The amazing insect only lives for three or four days in the entire year, during which time it must find a very specific host – the long-leafed wattle. It lays fifteen to twenty eggs in a flower bud in January, where they remain dormant until September – a time when the bud would normally become a flower. Then the eggs hatch and the larvae se-crete a chemical which mimics one of the plant's hormones, causing it to produce calloused tissue around the larvae. This aborts the flower and gives the larvae a wonderful home in the form of a tough green berry-like gall.

The larva pupates and by January turns into an adult wasp, which chews its way out of the gall. The tree has effectively been persuaded to produce wasps instead of seeds!

The wasp then has just three or four days to go in search of a suitable flower bud in which to lay its eggs and repeat the cycle. Little wonder that only a few people have ever seen the wasps, although the effects of their presence are clearly visible.

The adults are mostly females (90%) and can produce progeny without mating. This is a somewhat distressing concept for us males to come to terms with, and really doesn't bear thinking about!

Cape Times, May 1, 1998

The Pipe Track

Easy access to breathtaking views

Been thinking about hiking on Table Mountain but never quite got around to it? Well, this is the one to cut your teeth on. It's mostly along the level and with a view that compares favourably with the French Riviera, with towering peaks thrown in as a bonus.

The full Pipe Track from Kloof Nek to Slangolie Ravine above Camps Bay should take you three hours for the return journey. The obese, unfit and inadequate may take heart. You can turn back at any stage.

This is one of the best-known hikes in Cape Town and certainly one of the oldest, for the Pipe Track was constructed in 1887 to lay the pipeline from the proposed reservoirs on Table Mountain to Kloof Nek. Work began in the same year on the Woodhead tunnel, to which the track leads.

Start from Kloof Nek, next to the fire hazard board, and follow the steps up to a point where you will get a first look at the pipe crossing a small ravine. This is known as Blockhouse Aqueduct, named after a long since demolished blockhouse and gun battery built in 1781

by the French. They were occupying the Cape at the time to protect the Dutch settlers against the English. It seems the Frogs would go to great lengths – even travel halfway around the world – to try and give the Poms a *klap*.

The second aqueduct is appropriately named Granite Aqueduct. Discourage your children (and some adults) from trying a tightrope act on the pipe. It could spoil the rest of your day.

Ten to fifteen minutes after starting you will find yourself below the Kloof Nek filtration plant. This was built in 1938 to treat water from Woodhead reservoir and gave Cape Town its first crystal-clear water.

Before 1938 the water that came from Cape Town taps was brown. Looking up at the imposing building, notice the cannon, probably a relic from the French visit.

Beyond the filtration plant the Pipe Track plunges into Diep Sloot, giving you some work to do as you make your way out the other side.

This five-minute climb is really the greatest effort you have to put in on the whole journey, which fol-

lows a level contour most of the way. Note the occasional benches at strategic viewpoints. You are *so* close to the city and yet the feeling of unspoilt nature and raw mountain is all around you. Surely there is no other large city with such easy access to nature and breathtaking views? Rio, Sydney, Hong Kong and Vancouver might not agree, but they don't hold a candle to Cape Town.

Carry on along the Pipe Track, glancing up at the upper cable station. This imposing structure was built as far back as 1929, and still watches over the cable company's proud record of its entire existence

without an accident. I once told this to a superstitious Irishman half-way up. He cursed me roundly for having told him such a thing, and spent the rest of the journey on his haunches, from where he couldn't see a thing.

An hour and a half should bring you to the end of the line in Slangolie Ravine, after a brief climb up some steep steps. Perhaps returning the same way doesn't appeal to you, but somehow it's different. If this is your first hike, you'll somehow be different too. You're going to want to do this sort of thing again.

Cape Times, July 16, 1994

Kanonkop

With ancient
"splashes of paint"

Capetonians are a bit like Parisians in a way – complacent and smug about the magic of their cities.

Ask a Parisian about the Eiffel Tower and the chances are that only one in ten has been up it. And no less so with the Cape of Good Hope Nature Reserve – more commonly (and incorrectly) known as the *Cape Point* Nature Reserve.

And here is *moi*, a typical Smugtonian, who hadn't set foot in the place for 10 years. *Skande.* But we put that right a couple of weeks ago with a most delightful foray into the nether regions of our undiscovered Peninsula.

The Cape of Good Hope Nature Reserve is only 45 minutes from the southern suburbs and perhaps an hour and something from behind the Boerewors Curtain (except Durbanville, which might take a bit longer).

The drive itself is worthwhile. The walk is the cherry on top.

But when you get there, don't expect herds of wildebeest sweeping majestically across the plains, the Hanging Gardens of Babylon or Krakatoa erupting.

This is a gentle place. If the truth be known, a desolate place, but a place with a charm all of its own. Animals are few; plants are astonishing in their diversity.

The easiest and shortest hike is to Kanonkop, a signalling post used by the Dutch East India Company to warn Simon's Town of approaching hostile ships. The 45-minute climb to the cannon is up a gentle gradient, but the descent is down a fairly steep path, also taking 45 minutes.

The walk should take about two hours from start to finish, with time for tea at the top and to admire the all-round view. Apart from a panoramic view of the reserve, you can even see Hermanus and Gansbaai, beyond Hangklip on the other side of False Bay.

Once at the cannon, notice the white and orange lichens on the rocks, looking for all the world like extravagant splashes of paint. These ancient and primitive organisms are in fact composed of two elements – an alga and a fungus, living together for mutual benefit.

This association is termed "obligatory mutualism", since it is thought that neither partner can live

alone. Lichens are able to withstand severe drought, very high as well as freezing cold temperatures, as well as high salinity on the seashore.

And yet they are extremely sensitive to air pollution. Often the presence or absence of lichen species can be used to determine the amount of pollution in an area. They are slow growing, managing only about one millimetre per year, but some species are believed to live for up to 4 000 years. By the way, it's "lie-kins" not, please not, "litchens".

When leaving Kanonkop for the return descent, remember that the cannon points the way. Don't be tempted to take the more obvious path in the opposite direction, un-less you wish to climb to the top of Paulsberg, a strenuous twenty to thirty minutes away.

To get to the start of this gentle and rewarding climb, go through the main gates of the reserve – after paying a modest fee – and travel 6,4 km before turning left to Bordjiesrif. Then 1,2 km along this road before turning left again. The start is 200 metres on and clearly marked "Kanonkop Trail".

There are at least two other interesting walks in the area, worthy of a return visit, and they are begging to be rediscovered in the near future.

Cape Times, July 30, 1994

Walk on the wild side – in suburbia

Via an arboreal bypass

Who would ever have imagined a series of verdant hiking trails alongside river banks in the Cape Peninsula *running smack through the middle of suburbia*? And you don't even realise you're in suburbia. Johannesburg pioneered this concept with the Bronkhorstspruit Trail, and now Cape Town has followed suit. Full marks must go to the local council of Constantia Valley for laying out, signposting and maintaining a series of eleven trails for hikers, joggers and horse riders. Most of them run alongside river banks and through green belts, and all will eventually be interconnected. Most are no more than a couple of kilometres in length. So no great effort is required. The more energetic can combine two or three trails as our party did, and finish back at the start. It is planned to open more than the existing eleven, and links between trails will be created.

The man responsible for the planning and layout is town planner Nigel Burls who was kind enough to take a few of us on a sneak preview before the official opening in a few days' time.

We started by combining three trails – the Alphen, Klaassenbosch and Diep River Trails – a circular route which would return us to our cars when the sun was over the yardarm. And what finer setting in which to partake of the amber fluid than the sun playing hide-and-seek through the new oak leaves. A watering hole of unquestionable pedigree is the Alphen Hotel.

The signboard just before the entrance to the Alphen Hotel shows the way, proceeding along a most pleasant green belt and river bank of the Alphen Trail. Before long you will notice indigenous trees which have had their bark stripped for muti by traditional medicine men from the townships. If it's done all around the trunk, it has the immediate effect of killing the tree. What's that about the goose that lays the golden egg? The authorities have now taken to painting a grey poison on the tree trunks with an appropriate notice next to each one.

Where trunks have been "ring-barked", the Natal Parks Board have come up with an interesting experiment which seems to be

working. They cut off a thin branch at the top of the tree, drill a hole above and below the missing bark, and graft each end of the branch into the holes. A sort of arboreal bypass.

On the Alphen Trail section you will receive much attention from dogs behind fences, voicing what is probably their owners' disapproval at the invasion of their hitherto undisturbed privacy. But it is after all a public open green belt. It just hasn't been used much before.

The only thing tiring about these trails is saying "good morning" to endless streams of joggers who have also discovered the green arteries of Constantia. Will somebody please tell me why they all seem to have such pained expressions on their faces? It's as if they definitely weren't enjoying what they're doing. But they must be, otherwise they wouldn't be doing it . . . Strange.

At a detention pond, the trail forks to the right and becomes the Klaasenbosch Trail, following the river of the same name. After passing through an Afro-montane forest and past some splendid houses, the top end of the trail comes onto Rhodes Drive. Until a route can be worked out through Cecilia Forest, the route to join up with the top of the Diep River Trail unfortunately has to follow the road for 1,5 km.

But the Diep River Trail starting at the top of Southern Cross Drive is worth the tar connection. This section is particularly pleasant, and a bird sanctuary is to be created in the reeds with wooden walkways to hides.

Once back at the Alphen Hotel, you no doubt will be drawn into the "Boer 'n Brit" to round off the trail. This delightful pub reflects in its name some of the history of the serene homestead and surroundings. The Boer War of 1899 tore the country asunder and, as in all civil wars, family loyalties were split. The Cloetes of Alphen were no exception. Henry Cloete, although of Dutch descent, acted as a British agent, entertaining Lord Kitchener amongst others. His beautiful wife, in true Victorian style, publicly supported him but privately had no intention of backing the British, and regularly passed on valuable information to the Boer forces. Messages were hidden in a hollow oak in the grounds for collection by Boer agents. So whilst quaffing an ale or three in the pub after your hike, realise that there's more to it than just a name.

Mountain bikes are not permitted on the trails and a pamphlet entitled "A Guide to the Trails of Constantia" is obtainable from the Local Council of Constantia Valley.

Cape Times, September 17, 1994

Kaptein's Peak

And the mysterious
ghost town above Hout Bay

For a charming bird's-eye view of Hout Bay this little gem is well within reach of the novice hiker.

All right, forget granny and the toddlers, but most people should manage the top of Kaptein's Peak (414 metres) without too much difficulty. You're on gravel road for more than half the distance, so the climb has to be gradual.

The road itself has passed beyond the point of no return. It is now so neglected that even the best 4 x 4 by far wouldn't make it. Nevertheless it has an interesting history. Some years ago I made exhaustive inquiries about the origins of this road and the long since abandoned radar station to which it leads.

I tried everyone from the Navy to the Maritime Museum at the Castle and the Military Information Bureau in Pretoria. But to no avail.

Until, that is, I spoke to Willem Steenkamp Snr, defence reporter for this newspaper at the time.

He suggested a very feasible explanation for the mysterious aura which surrounds the abandoned radar station.

In 1944 the man in the street had never heard of radar. The few who were in the know regarded it as a weapon which could win the war for the Allies. So, hardly surprisingly, the first radar station built in SA (and probably one of the first in the world) was placed on the red-hot top secret list.

It is known that in 1948, when General Smuts lost the elections, he ordered the destruction of a lot of top-secret files to avoid them falling into National Party hands.

The Hout Bay Radar Station was obviously one of them.

I eventually, more by luck than good judgement, tracked down not only the man who selected the site, Dr F J Hewitt, but also Captain A C Johnston, who built the radar station.

They claimed the site was probably unique in the world at that time because of its height above sea level, overlooking a major shipping lane.

The gravel road to this little bit of local history starts at the extreme top right-hand corner of the houses above Hout Bay Harbour.

Find your way to the very end of

Bay View Road, from where the radar station gravel road continues all the way to the top of Karbonkelberg. Your destination is Kaptein's Peak on your right at the start, opposite the Sentinel.

Leave the gravel road about thirty minutes after leaving your car, at a point where it widens to about three times its normal width and becomes very sandy over a stretch of about 25 metres. You will notice a clear firebreak on the left, which leads to the "Long Drop" – well worth a visit on the way back.

Follow the firebreak to the right, turning off it once at the crest of the hill to follow a faint path to the peak. Once there you will be struck by probably one of the finest views in the Cape Peninsula. Looking down on Hout Bay harbour is surely one of the jewels in the crown of the Fairest Cape.

Once you have uplifted your soul, return to the gravel road but this time cross it and continue along the firebreak to the cliff edge. The staggering drop must be all of 300 metres without touching sides. I have no fear of heights but I caught my breath the first time I saw it.

Were you to miss the turn-off to Kaptein's Peak on the way up, the road would eventually take you all the way to the top of Karbonkelberg and the abandoned radar station in about one-and-a-half hours.

Cape Times, September 24, 1994

Hell in Constantia

A beautiful *buitepost*

Why is it that so many beautiful places seem to be called Hell? There's Die Hel near Oudtshoorn and Die Hel above Porterville in the Groot Winterhoek Mountains. And suddenly hell has broken out in the very heart of Constantia.

It's diabolical. But this one is a dense green heaven just 750 metres down from Constantia Nek on the Tokai side. The start is at Bus Stop 7929. Why on earth a bus should want to stop there is quite beyond me, for there is not a house in sight – just a lush green, deep valley. An added bonus for beginners is the fact that it's only an hour's walk both ways along fairly level ground.

It was one of several *buiteposte* (outposts) established by the Dutch East India Company to supply timber for shipbuilding and repairs, as well as fuel.

Continually burning open fires were the order of the day for everyone from cooks to coopers. In those days they couldn't just turn a switch on or off. Koeberg Nuclear Power Station wasn't yet on the drawing boards – so the only alternative was to burn loads of wood. This forest became one of the pillars on which the Cape's timber supply depended.

Another *buitepost* was what is today known as Newlands Forest. But then it was called "Paradys". One line of thought goes that Paradys was named by the woodcutters because it was close to the fleshpots of Wijnberg, not to mention the Tap House at Driekoppen (today a UCT residence is on the site).

De Hel, on the other hand, was far from the basic pleasures of life, besides which it was right next door to Simon van der Stel, allegedly the most cantankerous, ill-tempered so-and-so in the colony.

A far more likely origin to the apparent misnomer is the Dutch *De Hellen*, meaning "The Slope".

The fleshpots and Van der Stel theory, although colourful, needs to be confined to the status of urban legend.

You will love this short stroll through dense forest in the heart of suburbia. So will your dog and granny. Even the toddlers will handle it if you carry them part of the way.

This green glade boasts about

250 species of plants of which unfortunately about one third are aliens, including some horticultural escapees. But according to an extensive survey done by Dr Clive McDowell, of the UCT Botany Department, they can in time be eradicated and the area returned to a microcosm of what Constantia must have looked like in Van der Stel's time.

The bird life is quite active for such a small area, with 66 species recorded.

Indigenous trees include wild olive, Cape ebony and common turkey berry.

The fact that there is an indigenous forest like this still surviving in metropolitan Cape Town – albeit slightly shopsoiled with alien plants – is quite remarkable. It is an outdoor museum and classroom offering the casual hiker excellent value for energy. Minimum effort for maximum hiking pleasure.

This is one of eleven urban trails being laid out by the Constantia Valley Local Council, which will soon publish a pamphlet briefly describing each one. No permit is necessary.

Cape Times, November 25, 1994

Brakkloof Ridge

Ou toppies
at war with the aliens

This gentle climb along the ridge looking down on Fish Hoek is a visual example of what happens if alien vegetation is allowed to spread unchecked.

The path literally takes you through dark tunnels, laboriously cut out of the dense hakea and rooikrans for hundreds of metres. Along the way there are numerous escape routes out of the tunnel with views of the Fish Hoek and Glencairn valleys.

Start the walk at Ravine Steps near the Fish Hoek traffic circle and finish at the end of Risi Road near the kaolin mine. It takes two-and-a-half hours. Leave a car at the end. On foot, the distance is about 5,3 km, but by road it's a little over three kilometres.

It doesn't take much power of observation at the beginning of the walk to notice the difference between the harmonious diversity of the fynbos which has re-established itself and the smothering, all-pervading domination of just two alien plant species. They both come from Australia. Rooikrans occupies about 70% of the dense thicket. Hakea takes up the rest.

The invasion used to cover the ground all the way down to the road but, thanks to the tireless efforts of the Fish Hoek Alien Vegetation Control Group, the tide has been turned.

This conservation group led by Tom Keen is made up mostly of pensioners who voluntarily offer their services to hack out alien vegetation to allow the fynbos to re-establish itself. They have had spectacular success with this small section of mountainside.

However, without wishing to sound ungrateful or even cynical towards their sterling efforts, my personal opinion is that hack groups work well on small areas like this, but in the overall picture they barely make a dent in the national problem,

The scourge of these alien plants is a very serious problem. They rob us of enormous amounts of water which would otherwise fill our dams (fynbos doesn't use nearly as much). And they are taking over the richest botanical region in the world.

When one considers that a very high percentage of medicines originate from plant sources, think

about the effects on the world at large if our 8 500 species of flowering plants in the Western Cape were to be replaced by just five or six alien weeds .In some areas, that's already happened. Like Brakkloof Ridge.

Plants that perhaps hold the key to cures for everything from AIDS to cancer have disappeared. Along with the water.

And what's being done about it? With respect to hack groups, they haven't got a snowball's chance in hell of licking the problem.

The only real solution is biological control. The use of insects and fungal diseases is showing spectacular results. All over the Western Cape this biological warfare is becoming obvious to even the unpractised eye. Notice vast stands of Port Jackson willow with large hanging brown "blobs" on them. This is a rust fungus, the Port Jackson's natural enemy.

The same devastation is being wreaked on the long-leafed wattle by a wasp which lays its eggs in the flower and aborts seed production.

One of the biggest problems is rooikrans. Here politics raises its ugly head. Bring in biological control to kill the rooikrans and a large proportion of the Western Cape's population will be deprived of fuel to cook their meals.

The problem is a never-ending one but the walk isn't. It's an inspiration to a small and dedicated group of *ou toppies* who really deserve recognition for their labour.

Cape Times, April 9, 1998

Devil's Pit and Boomslang

Dassies and elephants

Devil's Pit and Boomslang hardly sound inviting, but they are the names of fascinating caves in the mountains above Kalk Bay. I was amazed that an old hiking friend of mine with many years' experience of walking in the Western Cape was totally unaware that the mountains above Kalk Bay and Muizenberg are riddled with caves. In fact there are 67 in all with names like Musical Drops Cave, Aladdin's Cave, Surprise Grotto, Commemoration Hall and Spookgrot. It was in this cave system that seven boy scouts got lost in December 1994.

Boomslang Cave actually goes 150 metres right through the mountain from one side to the other.

Kalk Bay got its name from the days of Simon van der Stel when kilns were used to burn seashells to produce lime (kalk) for mortar, used in building throughout the Peninsula.

An ideal introduction to the area is to walk to the Amphitheatre via a delightful indigenous forest in Echo Valley (no relation to the Echo Valley on Table Mountain) and return through an even nicer one in Spes Bona Valley. You might not see many caves, but you will certainly get a "feel" for the area. The start is on Boyes Drive up some steep steps marked by a Silvermine Reserve signpost. The steps are directly opposite and in line with the Kalk Bay Harbour entrance. As you ascend the well-worn path, you look down onto the picturesque fishing harbour while stopping for a rest.

At the head of Echo Valley, should you stumble across Ronan's Well, do not be tempted to go too far into it. This cave is not for amateurs, but is interesting to look into, and it always has water. At the ripe old age of fourteen, I was convinced that my days had come to an end when I got stuck in this cave, well beyond what was then the official end! Since then it has been further explored, and at 400 metres is the longest cave in these mountains. It is also one of the most dangerous, as seven young scouts discovered; so don't even think about exploring it.

In this sort of terrain you are likely to see plenty of dassies or rock rabbits. They are said to be closely related to elephants, but somehow I've never been able to see the sim-

ilarity. The word dassie is derived from the Dutch *das*, meaning badger. Unlike most wild animals, they seem to keep what we would consider to be socially acceptable toilet habits. They use only very specific areas in which to defecate. In time, these latrines become quite large; one in the Cederberg measures some three metres across and is almost one metre deep.

Dassies are probably one of the most important mammals in southern Africa. Predators such as eagles, and carnivores like the ratel and caracal, are either totally or largely dependent on them as a food source. Even their latrines, especially in arid areas, provide ecological nuclei for insects and lizards and their predators. Flies, for example, are attracted by the moisture and food source, and lizards are attracted by the flies. It's hardly surprising that ecologists refer to dassies as a "keystone" species. An entire complex food chain would collapse without them.

These gregarious animals are extremely agile in negotiating steep rock faces. Their padded feet are well adapted to gripping smooth surfaces simply by sweating. The same principle applies when we lick a finger to turn the page.

You should be able to complete the circuit in three hours, if you forgot to take a torch. Otherwise allow more time to explore some of the fascinating caves in the area.

Cape Times, December 16, 1994

Smuts' Track

A ghostly encounter
on Table Mountain

As recently as three years ago, I think I met General Smuts. Or more correctly Field Marshall The Right Honourable J C Smuts.

But he's been dead for 44 years I hear you say. I know. But nevertheless I think I met him on Table Mountain – on the very path that is named after him – Smuts' Track. Okay, so you think Lundy has finally lost it. Too much sun. And I don't even believe in ghosts – but the circumstances were so bizarre as to have left me wondering ever since.

When I did this particular walk for the purpose of writing *Best Walks in the Cape Peninsula,* I was pressed for time due to publishers' deadlines, and was obliged to do it in the foulest of weather, by myself – which was foolish on at least two counts, but it couldn't be avoided. Publishers and printers just don't understand. It was absolutely hosing down with rain, the wind was howling and visibility was down to about 20 metres.

Suddenly, out of the mist, came an old man dressed in rain gear, so that I could only see his eyes and nose and grey *bokbaardjie* through his anorak. I called out to him and said: "I thought I was the only one crazy enough to be on the mountain today." He came closer. The eyes. The eyes were so piercing as to be unnerving. The similarity was stunning. He said rather incongruously: "Surprisingly mild actually." And then he turned and disappeared into the mist. As I write, I still wonder about that old man. Was he real? Was I affected by the extreme weather conditions? Or could it be that he was . . .? No, surely not!

Smuts' Track is a classic walk which is surprisingly strenuous, considering it was named after a man who regularly walked this route even when well into his seventies. It starts from Kirstenbosch and finishes at the Upper Cable Station about $4^{1}/_{2}$ hours later. You can take the cable car down to your waiting car, if you haven't forgotten to take R10 for the fare (at the time of publishing that had rocketed to R60), or if the weather forces you to take the boneshaking alternative down Platteklip Gorge.

The way up Skeleton Gorge above Kirstenbosch is always in

the shade of indigenous forest and is punctuated in a couple of places with ladders, strategically placed to ease your way over the tricky bits. Shortly beyond the ladders the route is forced into the river bed by the surrounding cliffs. Most times the river flowing down Skeleton Gorge is a babbling brook but occasionally after heavy rain it gives out a thunderous roar. At times like this, it should rather be left to fair weather.

One-and-a-half hours should see you to the top of Skeleton Gorge, after which follow the signpost to Maclear's Beacon – the highest point on Table Mountain and the Peninsula. After that it's a flat walk along the Table Top to the Upper Cable Station.

Apart from the odd ghost or two, at this time of year you might just come across the occasional snake. There is no need to be alarmed. Most people's fear of snakes should be put firmly into perspective. The threat of death from snakebite is remote, despite gross misconceptions in this regard.

Cape Times, December 23, 1994

Little Lion's Head

And wee
cuckoo spit

Remember those somewhat offensive signs that used to appear in public places saying *Moenie spoeg nie/Do not spit*? Well, they could have done with a few on Klein Leeukoppie a couple of weeks ago.

Klein Leeukoppie – Little Lion's Head – is not to be confused with Lion's Head itself. It is an almost perfect replica of the real thing and lies between Hout Bay and Llandudno. Or Llandudno and Sandy Bay, depending on which direction your thoughts lie.

Shortly after the start, on the nek between Hout Bay and Llandudno, you will encounter a large patch of renosterbos, just below the TV mast. This tough little shrub appears to be covered all over with what at first sight appears to be white flowers. On closer inspection they seem more like what I can only call spit balls. *Ag sies!* But I mean, that's really what they look like.

I took a sample to Dr Mike Picker at the UCT Zoology Department. (It was a toss-up between that and the Botany Department, but as it turned out my guess was correct.)

Apparently it's called *cuckoo spit* and has absolutely nothing whatsoever to do with cuckoos. It is in fact the product of a beetle, not surprisingly called the spittle bug. If you separate the spit ball with a twig, the owner of the bubbly home will be found inside. He is a green soft-bodied insect who moves sluggishly and is ill at ease when removed from his foamy home. His reticence is understandable, as he would soon die if exposed to the hot sunshine.

This fascinating insect feeds on the sap of the plant which is a fairly weak solution of sugars and salts. Which means it has to take in vast quantities to get any value for money.

Rather than gorge itself fit to bust, it passes most of the liquid straight through the system, but not before adding a foaming agent and some air. I know all about breaking wind, but this is ridiculous – to build a *house* doing it. The resultant foam not only provides a shelter from the hot sun, but it conceals the insect from its enemies.

Allow an hour to get to the top,

plus another hour to enjoy the truly panoramic view and get down again. Geologically the route up is a perfect microcosm of the Peninsula's make-up. Igneous granite at the base with sedimentary sandstone on top. The route is fairly clear until it reaches the bands of sandstone about halfway up. Then you just need to keep a sharp eye open for cairns (rocky beacons of small stones piled one on top of the other) to show the way.

However, a word of warning for those with a heights problem – the last ten metres are a mild rock scramble. Dogs would have a problem. So you might just have to miss seeing Sandy Bay from on high. You will, though, be able to look down on Llandudno all the way up.

Llandudno, surely one of the loveliest bays in South Africa, was originally part of a huge farm called "Sands". The first owner was one Johan van Helsdingen, to whom it was granted in 1824.

Not much happened for the rest of the century to what was then known as Kleinkommetjiebaai. But in 1903 a township was founded by a company calling themselves the Camps Bay Extension Estates, Ltd. The wife of the chairman was struck by the similarity of the place to a seaside resort she had recently visited in Wales – and so the name Llandudno was adopted.

Electricity only reached Llandudno in 1947 and water was always a problem in the early days. Baths were taken at the Camps Bay swimming pool. Look down onto this little seaside gem now and you will probably see more swimming pools than in Houghton!

Return by the same route you went up, returning to your car inside two hours.

Cape Times, December 30, 1994

Getting as high as an elephant's eye

But no silver reward

What do an elephant's eye and a silver mine have in common? Nothing at all really, except they're both misnomers for places of interest on the Silvermine Circuit hike, starting near the top of Ou Kaapseweg.

Elephant's Eye is a cave which, when viewed from certain parts of Tokai and Constantia, looks like the eye of an elephant's head formed on the skyline by this part of the Constantiaberg. And there's probably more silver in my grandmother's tea set than there has ever been in this particular silver mine.

By order of the "Here XVII", shafts were sunk in the area between 1675 and 1685 but, alas, not one ounce of silver was ever discovered. Some people just never learn. Like the gold mine on Lion's Head. Greed is an all-consuming thing.

There are not many hikes left, with the hazards as they are, that can end with a bed of hot coals and a cold Castle. The vision of the sizzling chops and the amber fluid kind of gets you up the hills that much faster. The reservoir setting, surrounded by pine trees reflected in the surface of the water, complete the picture.

Not that there is much in the way of hills, mind you. Most of the walk is along a gravel road, which makes the going a lot easier.

Allow three hours for the circuit plus an extra hour for the detour to Elephant's Eye cave.

On the other hand, if you're just "here for the beer", there's nothing wrong with doing the *inner* circuit in less than half an hour.

That way you get to saying you came for the exercise when really you didn't. And you can smell the boerie for most of the way.

Apart from the tranquil "Canadian Lakes" setting for the braaivleis, there are also glorious viewpoints en route.

One is from Noordhoek Peak. Surely this is the most photogenic view in all of the Western Cape? It looks down, as if you were in a helicopter, onto the full sweep of Hout Bay and beyond.

Splendid view.

The other remarkable view is from Elephant's Eye Cave with the Cape Flats and False Bay all the way to Hangklip framed in the mouth of the cave.

On leaving Noordhoek Peak, the road descends gently for about half an hour before sweeping to the right, into the home stretch.

At this point another gravel road joins from the left and behind, coming from the top of Blackburn Ravine above Hout Bay.

This is the "old road" to Hout Bay and you are on it. It went from the Tokai Forest, along this route, and down Blackburn Ravine into Hout Bay.

It could only have been used by pack donkeys and horses, as I cannot imagine ox wagons making their way down the steep slopes of Blackburn Ravine.

Some eight minutes down the "old road" you'll come to a T-junction, which is the fifteen-minute route to the Lookout Hut and a further ten minutes to the cave.

With the braaivleis and beer beckoning strongly, make your way down to the Silvermine Reservoir and its many idyllic picnic spots, especially on the northern banks. Its entrance is at the top of Ou Kaapseweg.

Cape Times, January 27, 1995

The Suikerbossie Circuit

A naturalist's heaven

Most people know the Suikerbossie Restaurant on the nek between Llandudno and Hout Bay. But far fewer are aware that it is the start and end of a spectacular six-hour circuit which takes in a very deep and narrow wooded ravine, loaded at this time of year with the very symbol of our glorious Western Cape – the red disa.

Myburgh's Waterfall Ravine follows what right now is a dry river bed.

It is a naturalist's heaven where majestic yellowwoods reach for the narrow slit of sky. In one place the two opposing cliff faces of the ravine are a mere five metres apart and yet they reach perhaps forty to fifty metres up.

Water trickles down off fine moss, like the strings of a harp. Red disas, one of our most beautiful orchids, abound in their hundreds between late December and early February.

It is a very special ravine, reaching back in time to another era when the earth was young and unscathed by civilisation. Please respect it, as if it were a holy place. For it is. It is sacrosanct, as for that matter are our exquisite mountains themselves.

Someone whose identity has been lost in the sands of time is recorded as having said: "Our presence in the mountains is a privilege, not a right. It is our duty to hand this natural heritage over to our next generation, undamaged by our visits. We are borrowing it from our children for just a short while."

Hackneyed and worn at the edges in conservation circles perhaps, but it delivers a powerful message.

The start of this walk is at the stone gate entrance to the Ruyterplaats Estate, where you will bypass the security guard by taking a path to the left of the gate marked "Public Footpath".

The sympathetic developers of the estate will give you access to the mountain through their private property, which, they should be assured, is appreciated by the hiking public.

A word of warning though – if you have a fear of heights, perhaps it's best you take a doddle along the Pipe Track. There are three

places on this circuit which might lead to a flood of abusive phone calls and letters to the editor. However, if you don't mind a mild rock scramble (no ropes needed) – no problem.

Also, as this magnificent walk is long and complex, it is impossible to give an accurate description in the mere 600 words of this column. Therefore don't attempt it without the 2 000 words used to guide you more accurately in *Best Walks in the Cape Peninsula*.

I find ants fascinating. On this walk you will see fynbos at its best. Stop and wonder at the ants' capacity to perpetuate the very existence of fynbos. Many species of fynbos employ ants to bury their seeds, thus protecting them against fire as well as from being consumed by rodents.

The plants persuade the ants to bury their seeds by producing seeds with a food reward in the form of an "ant honey" sac, which doubles up as a handle with which to carry the seed.

Some indigenous ants, attracted by the "ant honey", carry the seed off to their underground nest, where they consume the food reward. Once the handle or "elaiosome" as it is known, has been eaten, the ant is unable to get a grip on the hard smooth seed, so it remains where it is, safely underground.

Unfortunately there is a villain in the piece. The invasive Argentine ant doesn't quite play the game as nature intended it. The selfish bastard eats the food reward without doing the job. Rodents then come along and eat the seed *sans* elaiosome. Even worse, alien ants drive off or destroy the indigenous ants involved in this vital process. In areas infested by imported Argentine ants, many fynbos species have become locally extinct.

Cape Times, February 10, 1995

The Sentinel

Guarding
Hout Bay

Hangberg is not Gallows Hill, as its name might imply. But a frightfully suitable place for a suicide, if you care to go the trouble of climbing it.

Not that I am suggesting such a dreadfully final solution to this month's telephone account. But the sheer drop from the top of the Sentinel guarding the entrance to Hout Bay is utterly breathtaking. Whoever changed its name from Hanging Mountain to the Sentinel simply had no idea of nomenclature, for this peak almost literally hangs over the sea on its southern aspect.

And as if to emphasise the point, there is a huge pile of rocks at its foot – the result of the sheer face of the Sentinel having collapsed into the sea. As this probably happened thousands of years ago, don't be too concerned about a repeat performance the day you decide to climb it from the back of its neck.

In a previous column we talked about walking around The Sentinel in Hout Bay. Now let's look at walking up it. (Rather surprisingly, a shade easier than the circular route.) Start from the very top left corner of the township above Hout Bay Harbour. It's an easy climb to the nek

between the Sentinel and Kaptein's Peak, lasting about ten minutes, before you see the mysterious "other side", enjoyed usually only by tourists on pleasure launches.

From the nek, look down on Duiker Island – another misnomer, for there is hardly a duiker to be seen. The island is wall-to-wall seals; their territorial squabbling and barking can be heard even from this distance. At the nek take a sharp left turn to follow the faint path all the way to the peak. When in doubt, keep a sharp lookout for cairns (rock beacons) which will guide the way.

You should reach the beacon about one hour after leaving your car. And then – the *pièce de résistance.* Assuming you aren't afraid of heights, you can lie on your tummy on a flat overhanging rock and look almost straight down into the water, 331 metres below. Mind blowing – if that's what turns you on. It does me, I have to admit. Not to mention that it's a little unusual to watch a passing trawler or pleasure launch as a tiny speck from above. The good news for vertigo sufferers is that you're not exposed at all to your worst fears until

you're at the very top. And then you don't have to look. Just take a look the other way, glancing gently down onto Hout Bay and especially the harbour, which reminds one that this has to be the jewel in the crown of "the fairest Cape in all the world" (Sir Francis Drake). Looking down on the bustling harbour might cause one to wonder when it all started. Commercial fishing as such probably began in Hout Bay in 1867, with the arrival of German immigrant Jacob Trautman.

On a trip some years ago to Mauritius, I was surprised to find large quantities of salted snoek for sale in Port Louis. Imported from Cape Town, what's more. Jacob Trautman had been sending our snoek to Mauritius well over a hundred years ago.

Perhaps one of the most colourful characters from those early days was Lucien Plessis. In 1903 he fitted out the barque *R Morrow* as a crayfish factory and his canned product was exported mainly to France. Needless to say, none was supplied to the local market. Eleven years later tragedy struck. An explosion caused by leaking gas ripped her apart, killing seven people, including Plessis himself.

This was a severe blow to the prosperity of Hout Bay, as the floating crayfish factory had provided employment for a large number of its people. The First World War broke out a few days later, and that spelt the end of Hout Bay's commercial beginning. The next major development was in 1936 with the building of the breakwater. This was perhaps the turning point in changing what was originally called Chapman's Chance from a sleepy fishing village into one of South Africa's most important fishing centres.

Cape Times, March 3, 1995

Above Boyes Drive

You take
the high road . . .

The mountains above Kalk Bay and Muizenberg must be among the most accessible and interesting in the country. There are many variations of short easy walks in the area known as the Silvermine Nature Reserve.

Most folk think of that as being confined to a small region at the top of Ou Kaapseweg, but in fact the reserve stretches all the way from Constantiaberg to Boyes Drive above Kalk Bay.

A delightfully scenic and non-strenuous climb starts on Boyes Drive above St James Station and when the route puts you directly above Kalk Bay Station, it gives you a choice. The lazy way or the keep-fit way. The high road or the low road.

The lazy way, of course, is to have another car waiting on Boyes Drive above Kalk Bay Station. The fit way is to walk back either along Boyes Drive (the low road) or via Hilltop Path (the high road).

Which reminds one of that wonderful old song with its origins buried deep in Scottish folklore – that I have sung out of tune and too loudly over many an ale at the club:

You take the high road
and I'll take the low road
and I'll get to Scotland before
you.

They believed that if a Scot were to lay down his life for his country in battle, his soul would return to Scotland immediately via an underground labyrinth of tunnels from anywhere in the world. That was the low road. The high road was on the surface for those who survived the battle. The normal and far more preferable way back to Scotland took a lot longer.

And so it is with the way back to your car in St James. The high road is preferable, although it does take a wee bit longer ($1^3/_4$ hours in total against one hour on the "low road" circuit).

Start at the Silvermine Nature Reserve signboard, at a kink in Boyes Drive almost above St James railway station. The path rises ever so gently, giving one the impression that Boyes Drive is dropping away below you, rather than you rising above it.

Within half an hour you will come to the end of a gravel road.

This is where you decide on the high road/low road option.

A left turn down into the little valley below will take you to Weary Willy's – a pleasant watering hole among some indigenous trees. A further left turn at Weary Willy's will lead you back to Boyes Drive in ten minutes.

Our decision to turn right and take the high road was prompted by a lady member of our party declaring with a sideways glance at her husband, that she'd seen enough weary willies in her life, and would give this one a miss. So it was that we took the high road.

If you decide to take the high road, walk along the gravel road for about twenty minutes before coming to a well-marked, clear path forking off to the right. This is the so-called Hilltop Path and marks the highest point of the walk. From here it's downhill. And about as gentle as it was uphill. After fifteen minutes on this path it will lead you down Bailey's Kloof and onto the zigzag path back to your car.

Cape Times, May 26, 1995

Blackburn Ravine

Blistering beauty

Blackburn Ravine above Chapman's Peak Drive in Hout Bay was named after the man who owned the land below it. But if the blister bushes are anything to go by, it should be renamed Blisterburn Ravine.

Once a week, I get a distressed phone call from somebody who has been climbing somewhere/anywhere on Table Mountain the previous weekend. The phone calls are invariably on a Tuesday or Wednesday, because the poison emitted by the blister bush (*Peucedanum galbanum*) takes 48 hours to start showing its effect.

Many a doctor has been fooled by these watery and tender blisters, because the patient who sees him on a Wednesday fails to mention that he was on the mountain last Sunday. That's a lifetime ago! Why should that have anything to do with blisters three days later?

And for that matter, the doctor can't be expected to make the connection either.

But it's a very real connection, so beware of these plants in Blackburn Ravine, or anywhere else on Table Mountain, for that matter.

How to recognise it? Quite easy. It has leaves like celery (it's also called mountain celery) and bamboo-like stems.

This interesting plant deserves healthy respect. Until recently very little was known about it. That was until Dr Natie Finkelstein of the Cape Technikon cast some interesting light on this indigenous plant.

It seems that a combination of slight bruising of the leaves, sunlight and time are the essential ingredients for blisters.

The substance exuded by the leaves is actually harmless. It's only when it is exposed to sunlight that it becomes poisonous.

So perhaps cloudy overcast days in midwinter are not such a bad idea for a walk on the mountain. And in sunshine, be sure to walk in front. You bruise the leaves, but those behind you collect the after-effects!

Start the walk on Chapman's Peak Drive, from the parking area 1,5 km past the Chapman's Peak Hotel.

Walk up the gravel forestry road in the direction of Hout Bay, until it doubles back on itself. Continue

on this road for about half an hour until it narrows and degenerates into an overgrown path.

Should you not be able to find the path as it turns the last corner into Blackburn Ravine, scramble up the small clay embankment above you, and there you will find it.

Stick to the path until it leads you into the densely wooded Blackburn Ravine and eventually to a small weir damming the river to provide water for the old forester's cottage near the start of the walk.

The elderly tree providing welcome shade at the weir is one of many examples in this ravine of *rooiels*, otherwise known by its English names of red alder or butterspoon tree. New leaves at the growing tip of each branch closely resemble flat butter spoons.

Retrace your steps from the weir. The so-called forestry road along which you have walked doesn't appear to have a forest. However, it used to be a thriving pine plantation, established in 1906. I can still remember it before it was destroyed by fire round about 1960.

Pines cause the soil to become acidic, which is much to the liking of fynbos, as evidenced by the many pincushions, proteas, cone bushes, ericas and many others which have re-established themselves in their rightful place.

Cape Times, March 27, 1998

WESTERN CAPE
MIDDLE DISTANCE

Moonshine and fynbos in the "grand palace"

Between Heaven and Earth

The mountains between Hermanus and the Valley of Heaven and Earth (*Hemel en Aarde*) must surely be "the grand palace" of the Cape floral kingdom.

So splendid are the unspoilt, rolling hills of pristine proteas that each time I wander down the corridors of this imaginary palace I regret not having done it more often.

The flowers and natural beauty here at any time of the year are quite special. The area has no less than three nature reserves abutting each other. Why not just one big one is explained by the fact that each is administered by a different authority.

Sounds like our education system of old.

The Fernkloof Nature Reserve is run by the Hermanus Municipality. Call (0283) 2-1122 for a permit.

The one in the middle is arguably the most beautiful, but Vogelgat Nature Reserve is privately owned and is not open to the public. You have to get lucky as I did and be invited as a guest of one of the 350 permit holders.

The third and most easterly one is Maanschynkop Nature Reserve and is looked after by Cape Nature Conservation.

Some of the names in this floral paradise conjure up mixed thoughts.

Shepherd's Camp and Leopard Camp are fortunately not too close to each other. On a hot day, Gurgle Stream, Froth Pool and Salvation Stream elicit just the right thoughts. Cookup Corner, Mist Gully and Moonshine Pass create their own pictures in the fertile mind, along with Shangri-la and Adder Ladder.

Mount Pustulata sounds utterly revolting, despite being named after one of the very beautiful ericas in the area, *Erica pustulata*.

And at the top of one uphill slog is a ceramic signpost, cemented to the rock, announcing that this place is called "Rest and be Thankful".

It's a joy to walk these mountains and find not one alien plant invader. Port Jackson, hakea and rooikrans are nowhere to be seen. The Hermanus authorities are to be commended for keeping this area so botanically pristine.

Seldom have I seen such a concentration and variety of fynbos in such a small area (the Fernkloof Nature Reserve is only 15 km but

it has more than a thousand species of flowering plants).

Fynbos (proteas, ericas and reeds), contrary to popular belief, actually *needs* a good fire every now and again. For many species fire is necessary to stimulate germination of their seeds. For fynbos to remain healthy and viable, it needs a good burn every ten to fifteen years. If no fire occurs within thirty years, the plant population begins to degenerate and become senile.

If, on the other hand, fires occur too regularly (more often than not they are caused by man), plants cannot reach sexual maturity to produce more seeds and the area soon becomes devoid of fynbos.

Within a short while alien vegetation (mainly originating from Australia) moves in.

From many points the view of the Walker Bay coastline is breathtaking – the full sweep is from Kleinmond past Hermanus to Gansbaai. You can even see the spot at which the troopship *HMS Birkenhead* sank in 1852 with the loss of 454 lives. It struck the rocks aptly named Danger Point and so began the maritime tradition of "women and children first" when abandoning ship.

So, if you haven't yet been in the "grand palace of fynbos", just do it.

Cape Times, May 8, 1998

The Limietberg Trail

Limit of civilisation?

The Limietberg, towering above Wellington, was named by the early settlers after they decided it was at the absolute limit of civilisation. Who knows, maybe it still is.

This fairly strenuous trail starts at the base of one well-known pass (Du Toit's Kloof) and ends at the bottom of another (Bain's Kloof). Botany and history fundis take note – your particular interests are here in abundance. Geologists too, on the second day, will be fascinated by the contrasting structure of adjoining peaks.

Start at Hawequas Nature Reserve, not far from the Nederburg Winery in Paarl and climb the gravel road to the top of Du Toit's Kloof Pass, named after one of the early French Huguenots – it was completed as recently as 1949, about two centuries after the good man had passed on.

Ever wondered about that narrow tar road that continues upwards from the top of Du Toit's Kloof Pass? Well, that's your route.

It will take you to the top of the range before you abandon it for a footpath to the right. The first day's walk is 18,3 km and will take about seven-and-a-half hours, finishing at a well-constructed hut overlooking the aptly named Happy Valley (it's lovely) through which flows the inappropriately named Witrivier (it's black).

On the way, you will cross a narrow concrete bridge straddling a deep furrow cut into the rock. This furrow, or channel, is interesting in that it was cut by a local farmer in 1856 to redirect the water from the Witrivier to the farms below.

Hugo's Rust, to which it now leads, has an interesting history of its own. It was a beautiful house built by Mr P J Hugo but was dogged by misfortune and Hugo died before he could occupy it.

In 1949 it was gutted by fire and became known as the *Spookhuis*. In 1978 a grisly murder of a young couple, by an escaped convict, was committed here and the ruins were subsequently flattened.

Enjoy your evening at the Limietberg Hut, beautifully positioned and equipped with bunks and mattresses, not too far – or far enough – from the *Spookhuis*.

Day two starts with a wander

through Bain's Kloof village – the small settlement at the top of the pass. It has a number of interesting features, including convict graves – a reminder of those who perished in the building of the pass between 1849 and 1853, and the ruins of the old Bain's Kloof Hotel, destroyed by fire in 1976. It served as a hitching post and *Eerste Tol* (First Toll) for what at one time was the only highway to the north.

From here the ascent of the Limietberg is long and steep but breathtaking in every sense. Despite the fact that this part was re-cently severely burnt, you could be rewarded with the sight of a rare protea (*P. nana*), rather incongruously known as the mountain rose.

Your end is *Tweede Tol*, a lovely picnic and camping spot with rolling green lawns at the bottom of Bain's Kloof, about 17,2 km (eight hours) from the overnight hut. Be sure to have left your car here, for it is 38 km back by road to Hawequas. Permits are obtainable from Cape Nature Conservation on (021) 889-1560/6/8.

Cape Times, February 5, 1994

Nature's perfumery

In verdant
Boegoekloof

The memory of beautiful Boegoe-kloof will long outlast the lingering fragrance of buchu which will cling to your clothes and body until that well-deserved shower, many hours later.

Boegoekloof, a deep, tight and beautifully aromatic green kloof, is part of the Hottentots Holland Nature Reserve through which runs the well-known Boland Trail.

It could almost be called a tributary of the Boland Trail, seldom visited by most, for it is only open during part of the year. To attempt it during midwinter would be foolhardy, as there would almost certainly be too much water in too narrow a ravine. But in summer at its upper reaches, you will hear the birth cries of the Riviersonderend – the main tributary of the Breede River, which it joins near Swellendam.

Boegoekloof can be visited either as a day trip from Hottentots Holland Nature Reserve (also known as Nuweberg Forest Station), just off the road between Grabouw and Villiersdorp, or as a weekend trail. The disadvantage of the day trip is that you need to retrace your steps all the way back once you have gone as far up the kloof as time allows.

The weekend alternative does the sort of justice to the kloof that it deserves – approaching from the top down rather than from the bottom up, and giving time to linger at majestic waterfalls and swim in deep dark pools.

Day one from Nuweberg to the Landdroskop overnight huts will only take $3^1/_2$ hours to cover the 10,6 km. But day two is a nine-hour half-marathon at nearly 21 km – strenuous, but worth every step.

The ubiquitous buchu, after which the kloof is named, is all pervading. The name comes from the Khoi (Hottentot) word for what is scientifically known as *Agathosma* (from the Greek *agathos* = good and *osma* = smell); indeed if you were to rub the small leaves between finger and thumb the pungent and aromatic smell would stay with you all day.

Buchu is closely related to oranges and lemons, and if you were to examine a buchu leaf under a magnifying glass it would resemble a citrus peel with its tiny oil sacs.

The Khoi sun-dried the leaves, reducing them to a powder which was either swallowed with water to cure stomach complaints or mixed with sheep fat and used as an ointment to heal wounds. It has probably been employed to cure almost every ailment known to man, and is still held in high esteem for its healing properties.

One of its better-known uses today is as a brandy tincture, but by far and away its most common employment came as something of a surprise to me on a recent chance visit to a buchu farmer in the Paarl Valley.

About 90% of his production is exported to Europe as distilled buchu oil, where it is used as a flavour enhancer for blackcurrant. Minute amounts of buchu oil (1,5 parts per million) added to blackcurrant makes it taste more like blackcurrant than blackcurrant! At higher dosages it has a similar magnifying effect on raspberry, strawberry and spearmint.

To visit nature's perfumery, book the Boegoekloof Trail by calling (021) 889-1560/6/8.

Cape Times, February 19, 1994

The Highlands Trail

Wild horses
and comfy nights

Kleinmond, between Hermanus and Betty's Bay, is pretty; but the mountains overlooking this coastline are even prettier with an abundance of fynbos and magnificent coastal vistas.

The Highlands Trail, with an overnight stop in the town, is really a combination of two one-day walks, making this weekend trail appealing to those who prefer a soft mattress and restaurant meal to Mother Earth after Toppers and Smash. A candle-lit dinner in a larney restaurant beats the hell out of trying to read the instructions on a soup packet by candlelight.

The Highlands Trail is a delightful mosaic of many things; pine forest, fynbos, lagoon, beach, rocky shoreline and mountain heights. All blend into a varied and interesting trail, full of surprises. Despite the distance travelled (33 to 36 km – depending on where you overnight), it is not a particularly strenuous trail and much of it is on fairly level ground, including an exciting lagoon crossing on day one.

One of your surprises might be to run into a herd of wild horses in the lagoon area. There are about six horses and their origin is steeped in mystery and contradictory local legend. Some say the horses' ancestors escaped from an abattoir (long since closed) and others say from a shipwreck. A more colourful version has it that their predecessors were hidden by the Boers from the Brits in the nearby mountains – hence Perdeberg, according to some. But it was named *Paardeberg* after the zebra, long before the Anglo-Boer War.

Unlike most hikes, this one starts at the top and works down. Park your car at the Highlands Forest Station and walk some three kilometres further on along the gravel road before leaving it to the left at Perdeberg picnic site, eventually arriving at the shores of the Bot River vlei. The crossing can be anything from ankle to armpit deep, depending on the time of year and how far your armpits are from the ground.

Once on the beach, the walk to Kleinmond and your accommodation is a shade over an hour. You will have booked your overnight stay beforehand, which could be anything from a recently upgraded three-star hotel to a rough-and-

ready municipal camp. Fortunately there is also a very pleasant compromise between the two extremes at Brightwood holiday cottages where my party and I stayed. Fully equipped cottages sleeping four, six and eight people work out quite reasonably per person. Facilities include a TV and swimming pool, but you need to take your own bedding, food and drink – phone (028) 271-3410 to book. A meal at the local restaurant is a bonus.

On the way to Brightwood you pass the Whistling Whale at the side of the hotel. Should you be tempted to pop in to wet your whistle, be warned that this most con-genial watering hole has caused many a trail to be abandoned 1 km from the end!

Next day, your walk back up the mountain is gentle (16 km/6,5 hours) and presents you with a remarkable diversity of ericas, proteas and birdsong. Not to mention the coastal views from on high. Don't forget to take a camera, binoculars and water. Strangely enough there is water to be seen everywhere, but hardly a drop to drink.

Permits can be obtained from Cape Nature Conservation by phoning (021) 889-1560/6/8.

Cape Times, March 5, 1994

The Postberg Wildflower Trail

The good things in life are done slowly

The Postberg Wildflower Trail is only open during August and September, so why on earth would this column deal with it in March?

The answer is simple: because booking opens on 1 April – that's next Friday – and if you haven't got in by 8 April, you can forget it.

The trail is extremely popular and limited to twelve hikers a day, so good luck, and enjoy it if you do get in.

The Postberg Wildflower Trail is wedged between the Atlantic Ocean and the Langebaan Lagoon, 100 km from Cape Town. This easy 21-km two-day trail is all about flowers, wildlife and birds – all in great profusion. The springtime flowers of the area are world famous, but the sheer variety of buck and birds comes as a surprise.

Some seasoned hikers feel it could be completed comfortably in one day. But that presupposes you are in it purely for the exercise and not to stop and linger, smell the flowers, spot the birds, try to get closer to the buck, watch a dung beetle at work or photograph a tortoise among the daisies.

All the good things in life are done slowly. This is one of them.

Overnight accommodation is under the stars alongside a beach with the uncomfortable name of Plankiesbaai. Take a lightweight tent and indeed hope that there *are* stars, for the campsite is right on the Atlantic coast and exposed to the full brunt of any inclement weather.

Given the right conditions, however, this is a good spot. It has an ablution block cleverly and inconspicuously built into a sand dune. As an absolutely last resort in foul weather, the cold concrete floor of a loo can be surprisingly comfortable.

Apart from the flower power, there is a remarkable amount of game to be seen including kudu, eland, gemsbok, springbok and wildebeest. Most of it, regrettably, is cautious and maintains a respectable distance and this is where binoculars come in handy.

The only animal that perhaps needs more respect than most is, oddly enough, a bird. Ostriches can be very nasty if threatened. They weigh up to 145 kg and run in excess of 45 km/h. The male is the black and white one, while the

female tends to be a uniform grey. During mating season, the male has bright red scales on the front of his legs which act as a major turn-on for the female and an equally explicit warning to other males.

Our eldest son, who works on a game farm in the Cederberg, could never understand why the male ostriches kept attacking his bakkie during mating seaon. It's red.

The moral of the story is, keep clear of ostriches sitting on eggs or looking after chicks. The male does half the incubating and sits faithfully on the eggs all night. The female takes over only by day, when her drab colour serves as protective camouflage.

Vondelingeiland (Foundling Is-land) opposite Kreeftebaai, which you'll see on the second day, was at one time covered with guano several metres thick. These were the heady days of the "Guano Rush" in the 1840s, when prospectors staked claims on the island after bird droppings were elevated from the unmentionable to the new-found respectability of being a valuable fertiliser. Until the 1950s, penguin eggs were collected and sold at the City Hall in Cape Town, to great demand. Try that now and they could just throw the key away.

To book for this delightful brush with nature, phone the West Coast National Park at (022) 772-2144.

Cape Times, March 26, 1994

The Genadendal Trail

This has one of the finest swimming holes

The ever-popular Greyton-McGregor Trail has become so popular that at certain times of the year it's difficult to get a booking. What a pleasure it is then to have an alternative trail in the area to fall back on.

The Genadendal Trail was opened in 1992 and soon became a favourite. But the unfit had best do a bit of homework first. This is a pretty strenuous trek over a formidable mountain range and back again by a different route; the Greyton-McGregor Trail is a cakewalk by comparison.

Find your way to Genadendal (approaching from Cape Town, turn left just before Caledon) and park your car in the quaint churchyard behind the delightfully unusual Moravian Church. Your vehicle will be out of place here, for you have just driven into the nineteenth century. The area surrounding the church has been lovingly restored to its former glory. A printing press, a restaurant and an old millstream add to the charm of the place.

As the first day is a long one (seven hours, 13,7 km) you might like to sleep over at Genadendal the night before. Accommodation is cheap enough at R10 per person in the old school dormitory. As a bonus you can arrange to have supper at the charming restaurant a few metres away from your lodgings. A mission station was established here in 1737 by Moravian missionary Georg Schmidt, the oldest in South Africa.

The trail starts from beyond the old mill on a path which zigzags up the steep mountain slope, relentlessly climbing for about two hours. Once over the top, you will soon reach an unusual rock formation known locally as *Wonderklippe* – finger-like columns of rock pointing skywards. After that it's mostly on the level or downhill. Pause to swim at Groot Koffiegat; one of the finest swimming holes to be found on a hiking trail.

Overnight accommodation is on the farm De Hoek on the opposite side of the mountains to Genadendal. Sleeping accommodation consists of six rooms of four bunks in each, but what makes this mountain hut a cut above the rest, is the "cookhouse". It's equipped with fridge, stove, gaslight and cooking utensils. Flush toilets and hot show-

ers are added luxuries. By prior arrangement the friendly farmer and his exuberant wife can sell you meat, bread, milk, etc., thus saving you the trouble of carrying it.

The return journey will take about six hours (11,6 km), but not before climbing a demanding slope for $2^1/2$ hours or more. It is absolutely essential to carry plenty of water on this second day, for there is none until halfway down the other side of the range. Once at the top, the amazing rock formations are awesome, not to mention the view of the other side.

At the end you cross the river and enter the back of the mission station the same way you started out. To book, phone Vrolijkheid Nature Reserve near McGregor (02353) 621 for a permit and De Hoek farm (02351) 2176 for accommodation.

Cape Times, April 23, 1994

Helderberg Farm Trail

Even
for Granny

Just off the Somerset West/Stellenbosch highway lives a farmer who has built a network of hiking routes on his farm. For a modest fee he will allow you to discover this charming getaway on the slopes of the Helderberg, near Somerset West. You can even spend the night on the mountain in a basic but comfortable hut.

In fact, this is an ideal hiking trail for beginners. It is as strenuous as you wish to make it, and even if you choose the most taxing option to Helderberg West Peak, it does not require a major effort. You have a choice of five routes, each with clear colour-coded footprint signs. The shortest is the so-called Green Route (1,8 km), which takes you through Granny's Forest. The name is appropriate for not only would Granny be capable of hiking it, she would be delighted with its old-world tranquillity. Apart from an uneasy alliance of indigenous and exotic trees, it contains seventeen species of fern.

Using the Granny's Forest route to get to it, the lower overnight hut is only fifteen to twenty minutes walk from the start, allowing you to use it as a base without needing to carry heavy gear very far. The hut nestles alongside a picturesque dam, which gives the pleasing illusion of always having been there. It's ideal for a dip after a hot day's walk, but if the weather or season doesn't permit this, then bird-watching around the dam could be a pleasant alternative.

From the viewpoint halfway up the slope can be seen the entire Cape Peninsula, both the Atlantic and Indian oceans and even Robben Island – something you don't expect to see from Somerset West. The multicoloured patchwork of surrounding farmlands and the profusion of proteas complete the picture. The proteas on the upper slopes are particularly pleasing, especially the ubiquitous sugar-bush (*P. repens*) and occasional green protea (*P. coronata*), not to mention the neighbouring protea farm growing mainly king protea (*P. cynaroides*) with the oleander leaf protea (*P. neriifolia*) on the boundary.

Every district in South Africa seems to have "The Big Tree". Helderberg Farm is no exception,

although this particular tree is not big in the sense of height (it's only eight metres), but it certainly has considerable girth and fullness. It's a rock candlewood, thought to be many hundreds of years old. Some experts feel it could be as much as a thousand years old. It's awesome to think that this tree was quite possibly well established at the time of the Battle of Hastings in 1066! What makes it even more unusual is that it is almost certainly the largest rock candlewood in existence.

The Helderberg Farm Trail can be done in part as a day walk or as a weekend option. To book, call the farmer, Wimpie Obermeyer, on (021) 855-4308. The cost of the overnight hut is minimal, and if you prefer to rough it in the shelter higher up the mountain, even cheaper. Firewood and braai grids are available at the base hut, which sleeps six people on foam mattresses. The shelter sleeps twelve on the hard floor.

Cape Times, May 7, 1994

The Vineyard Trail

Don't get lost
on a wine farm

Stellenbosch must be one of the most scenic and historic farming districts in the country and, thanks to the foresight of Stevie Smith, owner of Koopmanskloof wine farm, hikers are able to walk among this beauty and history.

His idea of a Vineyard Trail takes you past a series of koppies and ridges, through forest plantations, vineyards and olive groves – finally bringing you back to Stellenbosch, no doubt weary of limb but with a fresh appreciation of this beautiful land.

The Stellenbosch Information Bureau puts out a detailed map and brochure, showing different routes, each of which is colour coded red, green, blue or yellow. However, a number of these options involve a great deal of walking on gravel or even tar roads, which somehow takes the fun out of it. I recommend the "Blue Route" (you will need two cars unless you wish to walk the last six kilomtres on tar).

The recommended route is 17,5 km and should take about six hours including a short lunch on top of Bottelarykop. The route is reasonably well marked with colour cod-

ing, with a few notable exceptions. It might therefore be as well to go with someone who has done the route before. Nothing can be quite so fraught with temptation and undoing than getting lost on a wine farm.

The Vineyard Trail starts from the Oude Libertas Amphitheatre complex opposite Stellenbosch Farmers Winery, at the foot of Papegaaiberg (Parrot Mountain). It was here that Governor Simon van der Stel, in the early days of Stellenbosch, held an annual shooting contest in which the target was a wooden parrot. He established and gave his name to this charming university town more than 300 years ago.

Historic figures have been laid to rest in the nearby old cemetery, among them Dr D F Malan, a former Prime Minister. The trail climbs gently through a plantation of Monterey pines, which originate from California. Other aliens to be seen are umbrella pines from the Mediterranean and blue gums from Australia – not to mention the most welcome vines from Europe and America.

Once out of the forest and onto Papegaairant, you are treated to fine views of the Stellenbosch valley on one side and Devon Valley on the other. Two kilometres to the west is Fransmanskraal. This wine farm was so named when the French Huguenots camped there before moving on to their final destination of Franschhoek. To the right is the farm Goede Hoop (part of the Simonsig Wine Estate), which was a horse depot for the British Army during the Anglo-Boer War.

The most memorable feature of this trail is the breathtaking spectrum of colour. We hiked this area four weeks ago, and the autumn shades should rival even the New England states of the US in autumn. We tried describing the falling leaves with such mundane colours as brown, red, yellow and gold. And it didn't work. Aubergine and ochre, rust and oxblood seemed far more appropriate. Richer. More intense. No place here for mediocrity.

The trail is strenuous only in its length, for most of it is through rolling vineyards. There is however one steep half-hour slog uphill to reach the top of Bottelarykop and lunch in the welcome shade of pines. There is very little shade on the trail and no water at all; so be prepared and avoid midsummer.

The view from Bottelarykop is remarkable when one considers it is only 380 metres above the start. The entire Cape Peninsula from Table Mountain to Cape Point is clearly visible; as is the whole sweep of False Bay to Hangklip. On a clear day, you can indeed see for ever.

For more information, permits and a detailed map, call the Stellenbosch Information Bureau on (021) 883-3584 or 883-9633.

Cape Times, June 4, 1994

Paarl Mountain Nature Reserve

Gems at the back of beyond

The Diamond, the Pearl and the Tortoise. That's what the early inhabitants called the majestic granite islands in a sea of sandstone, standing like ancient monuments to the beauty of this place. Light rain or morning dew add to their glistening magnificence, to give the town below its name. Paarl is the only Afrikaans name I know which is not pronounced in Afrikaans as it is spelt. For "Paarl", say "Die Pêrel" (The Pearl).

The Paarl Mountain Nature Reserve will come as a surprise to those who were unaware of its presence high above the town. It covers nearly 2 000 hectares of mostly fynbos-covered plateau, and includes the three enormous rocks, with three picturesque dams adding to the tranquillity. Alas, two of the rocks have taken on other names as history has washed over them. They are now Bretagne Rock (after the French province), Gordon Rock (after Colonel Robert Gordon who commanded the British troops at the Cape from 1750 to 1795), and the smallest of the three is Paarl Rock, which hangs over those steeply sloping vineyards above the town.

There are many variations open to the hiker in this lesser-known nature reserve. Even the lazy and idle can drive around most of it. But the route which probably gives the best value for energy starts just above the Victoria Dam and finishes at the Meulwater Wild Flower Garden. Allow three hours excluding Oukraal or four hours if you choose to include it.

Approaching Bretagne Rock (the largest) from behind gives it a brooding and sinister aspect. But turn around and see the Afrikaans Language Monument with the blue mountains standing behind like a massed choir in full song. The path leads you between the huge rocks of Bretagne and Gordon and through an indigenous forest of Breede River yellowwoods.

The climb to the very top of Bretagne Rock is an optional extra, which will take about fifteen minutes, with the assistance of a chain railing. The climb up the rock is not at all exposed and no more difficult than climbing a steep staircase. The view is your just reward. Paarl Rock by comparison is much easier to reach, but not nearly as

rewarding. Of interest on Paarl Rock, however, is an old cannon which used to announce the arrival of merchant ships in Table Bay.

When you reach the gate (where entering cars are charged a modest fee), you will have to decide whether you have had enough, or wish to spend another hour getting a look at the two larger dams, and Oukraal. In the early part of the twentieth century, certain local families made regular camping trips to the area. Among them were the Oukraalers – a group which included one Manas de Villiers, who was a whizz on the banjo and spontaneously composed new songs as he was playing. Think of him as you wander by, for this is the origin of the well-known "Oukraalliedjie" (Oukraal song) so familiar to many South Africans.

Your return route from Oukraal takes you down past the waterfall at Dronknes. One shudders to think of the possible origins of that name. A permit is not needed to walk this delightful area, but a detailed map is essential. This, along with a comprehensive description of the geology, fauna and flora, is obtainable at R1 per copy from the Paarl Publicity Association by phoning (021) 872-4842 or 872-3829.

Cape Times, June 11, 1994

The Strandveld Educational Trail

A trail for enquiring minds

How much do you *really* know about the birds and the bees? That is, apart from the embarrassingly obvious? You would be *amazed* at the intimate things that consenting flowers can get up to. Especially if you see a video entitled *Sexual Encounters of the Floral Kind*, which you will see if you book into the Geelbek Lodge, at the southern end of Langebaan Lagoon on the West Coast.

It's part of the deal with the Strandveld Educational Trail, run by the West Coast National Park. Well – perhaps "run" is too strong a word; for the trail is a stop-start ramble from beginning to end. This is not a trail for the intrepid mountain hiker whose main aim is to conquer peaks. For there are none.

Both days of the walk are over fairly level terrain, mostly following a rough four-wheel-drive track. However, if you are sufficiently interested, you will learn more about nature and your environment on this trail than on any other I know of. This is a trail for birders and those with a botanical bent, and anyone else who wants to know more about the delicate balance of nature.

Accommodation is at the Geelbek Environmental Centre, your gracious Cape Dutch home for two days. Situated on the Langebaan Lagoon an hour's drive from Cape Town, this beautiful bit of Cape chronicle has accommmodation for up to thirty people in dormitories. Double bunks are fitted with sheets and duvets and wholesome West Coast meals are served in the dining room which also has bar facilities. This is definitely at the luxury end of the hiking accommodation spectrum; in a setting that just reeks of history.

The purpose of the weekend is environmental education. If you're not into that, then don't bother. You might just die of boredom. But if you are, the Strandveld could blow your mind. National Parks Board officials will show you films, give you short lectures and then debrief you when you return. You will learn about *gifmelkbos* (poison milk bush) and how buck eat it with impunity. And how birds use *kapokbos* to give their nests a luxurious lining. You will also discover how an ostrich bathes – not in water but in a dustbowl, and why.

You will meet the dung beetle, which has been known to eat more that its own weight in dung in 24 hours. In fact, you will discover many wondrous things if you go slowly and observe carefully, using the excellent guide booklet handed out by the National Parks Board. The faster you go, the less you will see. But you can't miss the deep footpaths in the sand or grass made by rats and mice crossing your route. Considering the speed at which these creatures scurry to and fro, I prefer to call these race tracks "rodent highways".

The highest point of the trail is all of 35 metres above sea level. But perhaps the high point of the trail on a hot day is the swimming hole. It stretches from Sixteen Mile Beach all the way to Argentina.

To book the Strandveld Educational Trail call or fax (022) 772-2798/9 and push your luck for a springtime booking. If you don't ask, you don't get. The cost of the weekend, inclusive of meals, lunch packs and accommodation was R150 per person at the time of writing.

Cape Times, July 23, 1994

SAS Saldanha Hiking Trail

Wall-to-wall carpet stuff

Did you know that the Mother City was once called Saldanha Bay? Well near enough. *Agoada de Saldanha* – the watering place of Saldanha. In 1503 Portuguese commander Antonio de Saldanha left Lisbon on a journey to the Far East with a small fleet of three warships. He soon not only lost contact with his other two vessels, but lost his way as well. Some months later he stumbled into Table Bay and named it *Agoada de Saldanha*. For nearly a hundred years charts bore this name.

Then along came Joris van Spilbergen, a Dutch explorer who was even more confused than the Pork & Cheese. In 1601 he made his landfall too far north and found what he thought was *Agoada de Saldanha*. After a few days he proceeded further South and discovered what he believed was a completely new bay with a fascinating flat mountain, which he named *Tafelberg* and *Tafel Baay*. The fact that Saldanha never clapped eyes on Saldanha Bay or even knew of its existence doesn't seem to bother anyone. Least of all the sea dogs who have created the SAS Saldanha Hiking Trail.

Do this trail now – this weekend. Or at the latest in the next two weeks. Our group did it two weeks ago and the spring flowers were utterly breathtaking. Wall-to-wall carpet stuff. But that's not all. Herds of springbok cascading over the road ahead of you. Seabirds that have no idea of what birdsong is all about. And ostriches weighing up to 145 kg.

If it's flowered, feathered, finned or furred, it's here on the SAS Saldanha Trail. A variety of routes are offered ranging from four to 15,5 km. The Green Route done by our party seemed to present the best of all things, and is 11,5 km, taking us an easy four hours.

The "SAS" part of the name stands for South African Ship. Which is a bit odd because there's certainly no ship to be seen on this trail. But in naval parlance a "stone frigate" is a shore-based training establishment, made of bricks and mortar.

One of the most famous ships in Saldanha's fascinating history was the American raider, *Alabama*. In the American War of Independence, fighting for the Confed-

erates, she sank 75 Yankee ships and became the most feared vessel afloat. On 29 July 1863 she steamed her way into Saldanha Bay to undergo running repairs.

The captain was surprised to find such a magnificent deep-water harbour totally unoccupied. Soon the news of her presence so close to the shipping lanes of the Cape of Good Hope spread, causing a sensation in Cape Town. On 5 August 1863 she weighed anchor and set sail for Cape Town where it had been established she could take on fresh supplies of victuals and coal.

Cape Town buzzed with excitement at the impending arrival of this famous raider. In full view of thousands of spectators on Signal Hill, her arrival in Table Bay coincided with the arrival of a Yankee barque, the *Sea-Bride*. The latter, to the delight of the watching audience, was promptly snapped up as a prize of war. To this day in the Cape they still sing "Daar kom die Alabama".

Saldanha's perfect natural harbour could easily have led to Cape Town being where Saldanha is today, were it not for a complete lack of water to support a large city. That doesn't seem to bother the flowers, though, so hurry up and enjoy them while they last.

Call the stone frigate on (022) 702-3999. And in this day and age it is refreshing to find that there is no charge for the permit. So the best things in life are indeed free.

Cape Times, September 10, 1994

Koeberg Nuclear Power Station's Dikkop Trail

Take a walk on the nuclear side

Guy Fawkes day is hardly the time to read about hiking around nuclear power stations. The implications are overpoweringly insensitive. But forgive me: I'm on a mission. "Atom" *is* a four-letter word, but not *nearly* as bad as some I've heard – and used.

Man has been around for five million years, give or take a long weekend. And yet he has only made use of electricity since the last century. Now he can't do without it. Like automatic pool cleaners and garage door openers. You can do without them until you've had one.

There are only three major ways of meeting the basic electricity demands of the modern world; by making use of water, coal or nuclear fission.

In South Africa water resources are unreliable. Our coal reserves are only expected to last until the middle of the twenty-first century. And that's just around the corner. Apart from which the combustion of coal presents a serious threat to health and the environment. Harnessing the wind or solar energy or even geysers (which we don't have

anyway) are pathetic possibilities compared to the needs.

So what's left? Only one thing, so you had better get used to the idea. Nuclear fission is not the bogeyman it's been made out to be by people who simply don't know the facts. One kilogram of uranium supplies the same amount of energy as three *million* kilograms of coal. Uranium is more abundant than gold and silver . . . and so the surprising facts go on. But more of those next week when the threat of Guy Fawkes has worn off. Don't even mention Chernobyl. Let's get on with the trail.

Koeberg Nature Reserve, created in 1991 by an environmentally sensitive Eskom, has two hiking trails. There is the Dikkop Trail and the Grysbok Trail. They lead the hiker through the two naturally occurring veld types in the area – the Dikkop Trail through a superbly healthy example of strandveld and the Grysbok Trail through dune veld. The former is thirteen kilometres (four hours), or eight kilometres (three hours) depending on the route you choose. The Grysbok Trail also has two options of

2,5 km and 4,4 km.

The Dikkop Trail starts a few hundred metres past the Atlantis turn-off on the West Coast Road, and proceeds mainly along sandy track to the coast through some very green and surprisingly lush strandveld. The highest point you will reach is only 71 metres above sea level, so this is not a peak-bagging exercise – merely a stroll through the strandveld. But with soft sand underfoot, that in itself can be tiring. On Tuesday you could find aching muscles you had forgotten you had.

While treading this soft dry sand, it will be hard to imagine that not far below your feet is what Koeberg claims is the largest sand aquifer in the world. An aquifer is an underground lake and it pro-vides all of the 60 000 inhabitants of Atlantis, plus all industry in the area, with five million cubic metres of fresh drinking water a year. The capacity is thought to be much more than that. Nineteen million cubic metres every year just runs into the sea, if you please. Where on earth it comes from on the arid West Coast, heaven only knows.

To book, call the Koeberg Nuclear Power Station on (021) 553-2133 and, if you go on a Sunday, try to coincide your hike with the visitors' centre being open on the second and last Sunday of each month. The educational value of the models on display is worth a visit all on its own.

Cape Times, November 5, 1994

Koeberg Nuclear Power Station's Grysbok Trail

A plot to confuse the barnacles

Try to imagine the awesome size and power of pumps that can empty two large domestic swimming pools in just one second.

That's the equivalent of the 80 000 litres of water which is pumped every second of every day to cool the massive condensers of the Koeberg nuclear power station. Fortunately the source of this huge amount of cooling water is endless, for it is the Atlantic Ocean.

But this brings with it other problems. Barnacles and mussels which normally feed on the plankton twice a day when high tide brings it in are now in their seventh heaven: with two swimming pools of plankton-carrying water coming past every second, it's feeding time all day and all night. Wonderful. Except the mussels become enormous in no time at all. In huge numbers they would reduce the inlet pipe diameter, thus reducing the water flow and cooling capacity of the plant.

The implications of an overheated nuclear plant don't bear thinking about so, to avoid this, shock doses of chlorine were introduced into the inlet lines at regular intervals. But in the early days of sea-water-cooled plants it was soon discovered that the mussels and barnacles appeared to have developed a resistance to the chlorine. So dosage levels were drastically increased, but to everyone's surprise, to absolutely no avail.

Eventually divers were sent down to investigate and what they observed was stranger than fiction.

These lowly creatures have no brain as such, and certainly no level of intelligence. Yet a couple of minutes before each scheduled chlorination, they literally "closed up" and held their breath until the danger had passed.

They knew exactly what time it was!

Now all nuclear plants chlorinate at random times, without sticking to a fixed schedule. Catch the little perishers with their pants down, I say.

Last week in this column we discussed the Dikkop Trail at the northern end of the Koeberg Nature Reserve. There the typical vegetation is strandveld. For those who want a really easy one-hour stroll, there is the Grysbok Trail, south of the nuclear reactor. Here the vege-

tation is duneveld, with an ecosystem all of its own.

Margaret Thatcher said the challenge of the 1990s would be the environment. Eskom has certainly taken this challenge seriously with an ongoing programme to eradicate alien vegetation and reintroduce indigenous species along with a wide range of fauna from bontebok to ostrich.

The Grysbok Trail starts at the visitors' centre, which is an absolute must. It is open Monday to Friday, but not Saturday. If you choose to walk on a Sunday, make sure it is the second or the last Sunday of the month, when this fascinating educational museum-type centre is open.

The trail is well marked and gives you an option of 2,5 km, or if you do the extra bit to the beach, 4,4 km. No big deal, and not even uphill. But what you will learn about the environment and nuclear fission will surprise you.

Should you be worried about exposure to radiation, forget it. You will be exposed to more radiation by taking a two-hour flight to Johannesburg than if you were to sit on the perimeter fence of Koeberg for one year, naked. You'd probably get pretty cold, but you'd be far better off than frequent fliers.

Cape Times, November 12, 1994

The Boland Trail's Orchards Route

Two contrasting days

The Boland Trail has a disquieting record in the annals of South African trails. Seven people were killed in the first eight years since it was opened in 1976. Eventually it began to dawn on the authorities that something wasn't quite right, and about five years ago they closed the offending section from the top of Sir Lowry's Pass to Landdroskop Hut. The cause of death in all cases was the Western Cape's unpredictable weather. Starting off with clear blue skies is no guarantee that six hours later you won't be inside a cloud without a jersey in subzero wet and windy conditions. Respect the mountain, or it will have no mercy on you.

Nowadays the Boland Trail is divided into bite-sized sections which are far more user-friendly. One of these is the so-called Orchards Route, a two-day circular hike, overnighting in wooden huts at the terminal point in Boesmanskloof.

Day one is quite strenuous, but the strain is relieved by three good swimming holes along the way, with another at the end. Day two is as different from day one in scen-

ery and terrain as day is from night. And, strangely, the return route is merely on the other side of the same mountain range.

Whereas day one might have been a strain for some, amidst grand scenery, seemingly cut off from civilisation, day two is a piece of cake. For most of the return route an easy 400-metre contour is followed, overlooking verdant farmlands rich in apple orchards – an entirely different scene and most pleasing to the eye. The patchwork of orchards, separated by lines of pines with the occasional farmhouse, presents a pretty picture.

The start of the hike, as well as the other sections of the Boland Trail, is the Hottentots Holland Nature Reserve, previously known as the Nuweberg Forest Station, situated just off the main tar road between Grabouw and Villiersdorp.

Incidentally, the name "Hottentots Holland" was originally applied to the bowl below the mountains occupied by present-day Somerset West. The Khoikhoi (Hottentots) living in the area at the time, told the Dutch Settlers that this was their

home – their "Holland".

Along the way, not far from Red Hat Crossing, you will probably see a sign showing the way to Suicide Gorge. Unless you have tendencies in that direction, best ignore it. It is a kloofing trail strictly for mountain yuppies.

I shall never forget jumping off an eighteen-metre cliff (the same as a six-storey building) into an inky black pool, just to prove to my son that I wasn't absolutely petrified. I hit the water like a badly unbalanced elephant at terminal velocity and finished up with a bloody nose and dented pride, despite being eternally grateful to be alive. My son is forbidden to discuss the incident.

Accommodation at Boesmans-kloof is in wooden huts. Basic, but more than adequate. Each sleeps about thirty hikers.

Among the highlights of this trail are three long suspension bridges. Be sure to cross one person at a time, otherwise you might learn the hard way why army troops "break step" when crossing a bridge. The added weight of extra people is not a factor. The harmonic frequency set up by just one person's footsteps on a suspension bridge like this is most noticeable. With two or more people walking in step the effect is remarkable, if not dangerous.

To book this trail (permit required) call (021) 889-1560/6/8.

Cape Times, January 6, 1995

Jonkershoek Traverse

From photogenic
to Fanie's Folly

The azure blue mountains of the Jonkershoek Valley near Stellenbosch must surely be one of the most photogenic ranges in the country, outside of the Drakensberg. They stand proudly in their rich blue uniforms that no-one else is privileged to wear. Lesser mountains are a drab grey, clothed only in patches of green.

Even if you don't climb them, they are worth a look. The Jonkershoek Valley is only ten kilometres out of Stellenbosch on a dead-end road winding through lush scenery to this little heaven. Try it sometime.

The first settler in these parts was one Jan Andriessen, a German ensign in the employ of the Dutch East India Company. The Dutch for ensign (or lowest ranking infantry officer) was "jonker" (derived from *jonk heer* or young gentleman). So in much the same way as one might expect to find Jones the Coal in Wales, he became known as Jan de Jonker – hence the name Jonkershoek.

Not only does this valley offer some delightful day walks, but it is also the end of a fairly strenuous two-day route which bisects the Boland Trail from south to north.

Starting at Nuweberg between Elgin and Villiersdorp, the walk follows a fairly easy route on the first day to the Landdroskop huts. The 10,6 km of day one takes less than four hours and ends at these two well-known huts.

You may well be tempted to ask why there are two instead of just one big one. The answer is that they are a legacy from apartheid. Rather ironically though, the authorities, attempting to favour whites, got it the wrong way round. Shamrock Lodge, which was supposed to serve as the "dark green" hut, is in fact cosier, warmer, lighter and less cramped than the supposedly better Landdroskop hut. The latter has been irreverently referred to as, among other things, Cape Town Station, alluding to how crowded it always seems to be, even when it's only half full, despite its larger size.

Another unflattering name given to this cold stone edifice is "Fanie's Folly", after an erstwhile Minister of Forestry, Fanie Botha, who is said to have designed the building on the back of a cigarette box.

The braai grids and fireplaces in

the outside kitchen areas of both huts have been removed. Why, you might well ask? A good enough reason. When the firewood, supplied free of charge by the authorities, ran out, people started breaking up the bunks to use as firewood. Can you believe it?

Day two of the trail, although only a bit longer, is more strenuous. Plan to have lunch at Pic-sans-nom (meaning peak without a name). The view from here is dramatically sudden and quite exceptional. The entire Helderberg amphitheatre spreads below you, with Gordon's Bay, the Strand and the full sweep of False Bay completing the picture. A final gift at the end of the trail, after a long downhill wobble, is a rather pleasant swimming hole. Pity it can't be moved up to Pic-sans-nom and they could call it Goef-sans-Cozzie.

Obviously one needs to leave transport at the end of the trail in the Jonkershoek Forest Station, but the exercise is a time-consuming one. Allow at least $2^1/_2$ hours between leaving Cape Town and actually commencing the walk from Nuweberg.

To book phone the Cape Nature Conservation booking office at Jonkershoek – on the Cape Town exchange at (021) 889-1560/6/8.

Cape Times, February 17, 1995

Tygerberg Nature Reserve

A tiger with spots?

There is life behind the Boerewors Curtain. In fact, there are surprisingly scenic hiking trails right in the middle of suburbia. And where might the Boerewors Curtain be, you may ask.

Well, like the Iron Curtain and the Bamboo Curtain, you can't actually see it. But it stretches across the N1 more or less opposite the N1 City shopping centre. And you can definitely smell it; especially on Sundays after the sun has passed over the yardarm.

As one who has lived in the southern suburbs most of my life, I've always been under the dreadful misconception that us okes in the shadow of Mother Mountain are the ones who are blessed with all the pleasant walks in the Western Cape. Wrong, wrong, wrong.

Right in the heart of a densely populated area between Welgemoed and Plattekloof (an area often described as the Constantia of the North) lie the Tygerberg Hills. And right there on top is the Tygerberg Nature Reserve. Wow! Who would have believed it – grysbok, porcupine, tortoise and renosterveld – in the not-so-small enclave just four kilometres off the National Road. This 67 hectare reserve not only boasts panoramic views but 158 bird species as well. There are no less than forty species of butterfly here, with four of them on the endangered list.

Despite being proclaimed a nature reserve as far back as 1972, surprisingly few people in Bellville, Durbanville and Parow seem to be aware of its presence. A charming "old"-looking building (built in 1991) at the entrance gate was originally intended for educational purposes, to teach nature conservation and the like to schools and clubs. But the vacuum has been filled, alas, by big business, which is using this wonderful facility for seminars. Money, not the love of nature, has taken charge.

Desperate to change the situation is curator Ken Warner, who would just love to teach school groups about the Great Outdoors. If you are a biology teacher, it's your duty to your pupils to give him a call right now, on (021) 913-5595.

There is a myriad of clearly marked paths throughout the reserve and you can choose to walk

any one of the many routes, which will take you anything from ten minutes to two hours. The highlight of the reserve is the look-out point, which gives a wonderful panorama of Table Bay, False Bay, the Hottentots Holland Mountains and much, much more.

The name Tygerberg does not indicate that some Bengal tigers found their way to this part of the world. "Tyger" seems to have been the somewhat confused Dutch word for the leopard. So what, if a few spots were mistaken for stripes! Areas of fallow grass interspersed with the grey-green fynbos give the hills a spotted appearance when seen from a distance. It is these spots which gave the Tygerberg its name.

Cape Times, June 16, 1995

WESTERN CAPE
FAR AWAY

The Harkerville Trail

We meet
the Hound of the Harkervilles

The Harkerville Trail lies deep in the forest midway between Knysna and Plett. It's also halfway between Paradise and Purgatory.

Paradise is the indigenous forest where the silence is deafening, punctuated occasionally by the call of the Knysna loerie. And paradise is the forest floor carpeted in a dense layer of green fern, interrupted now and then by a bright orange bracket fungus and a gurgling silver stream. Purgatory is the cliff faces you have to negotiate, using ladders and chains. If you have no head for heights, then this is when you discover that the colour of adrenaline is brown. Not a pretty sight. But then Purgatory is, after all, only a place of temporary suffering – and soon it's back to Heaven.

Our hiking group did this trail two weekends ago. We were originally known as the Houtbaai Voortrekkers but we changed our name, all being English-speaking, to the Wood Bay Frontpullers. Anyway, off we set, accompanied by the forester's dog which apparently makes a habit of accompanying hikers on the two-day walk. This amazing bitch is a cross between a Rottweiler and a Doberman. Absolutely huge but still a galumphing puppy at one year old. We strongly suspected there was a large dose of mountain goat in her ancestry, because she was incredibly agile for such a large animal.

At one time on the second day, we feared the worst. Confronted by a sheer cliff face on the one side and the thundering white sea on the other, we wondered how on earth we were going to get her up the seven-metre chain ladder which was dangling down the face. We went into a huddle to discuss constructing a makeshift sling, only to find the beast looking down on us from the top of the ladder. Heaven knows how she got up there, but it wasn't via the ladder.

Although worlds away from Dartmoor and the Baskervilles, she became known as the Hound of the Harkervilles. Sheba is her real name. But don't worry about her if she latches on. She knows every step of the way, including some miraculous way around the ladder, which we couldn't find.

If the nearby Otter Trail is said to

be the prince of trails, then I've always claimed that the Amatola Trail in the Ciskei is the king. While the Harkerville Trail might not be quite as deserving of such accolades, it is clearly a member of the royal household of hikes. The coastline is breathtakingly wild and untamed. Huge rocky needles stick straight up out of the sea, guarding the coast like so many sentries. This is definitely not a place you would choose to get shipwrecked.

It's a wonderfully varied hike taking about seven hours on the first day and six hours on the second. Overnight accommodation is in a pleasant wooden hut with mattres-ses on the bunks only 25 mm thick. But you will be too tired to notice.

There's a surprise around every corner, including a stand of giant Californian redwoods planted in 1927. With a trunk diameter of 2,5 metres they are like the dog; just big babies.

Comments on the 26,6-km hike ranged from "a piece of cake" to "exciting" to "pretty hairy". It's all a matter of how much adrenaline you secrete. If you're worried about the chains, just remember it's not the fall that gets you. It's the sudden stop at the bottom.

Cape Times, June 26, 1998

Busch-whacking in the Langeberg

Close encounters of the third kind

I have no idea why I didn't write about the Pat Busch Trail when I first walked it in 1995.

I did it again a year later and the second time around was even better. The plants were greener and the rivers fuller.

You will be surprised by the trail, which is midway between Robertson and Ashton and about two hours' drive from Cape Town.

It's rich in fynbos, ferns and forests. Perhaps the fynbos is not surprising, but the indigenous riverine forests and the abundant ferns certainly are.

Pat Busch is a German immigrant who worked hard, did well and bought a farm in the foothills of the Langeberg.

In 1989 Busch opened his mountain retreat to the hiking public.

He chose to keep a low profile to attract the right kind of people by word of mouth – those people who would appreciate this beautiful little corner of the Cape.

There are a number of short trails on the farm, some of which Pat has named after his wife and children.

Appropriately and lovingly, the loveliest option is named after his wife, Karin. It is beautiful, especially when the rivers are running, as they are now.

We were also impressed by what we did *not* see – there was not a single alien invasive plant on the four-hour route we chose, except at the end when we stumbled into a forest of poplars and pines. I wasn't sure whether to be disappointed by their colonisation of a pristine area or grateful for the shade.

Talking of aliens – on our first trip, one of our number, not given to wild flashes of imagination, swears blind that she saw a UFO at three in the morning.

Her graphic description was greeted with howls of derision and mocking laughter – until the farmer told us there had been numerous previous sightings.

Visitors from other worlds aside, this is a restful weekend and quite within the capability of beginners.

Choose your own route; there are several trails which take from about thirty minutes to $4\frac{1}{2}$ hours to complete.

If you want a more strenuous weekend, you might like to combine

hiking with canoeing, as we did: we spent Friday and Saturday nights on Pat Busch's farm and Sunday with Felix Unite, canoeing down the rapids of the Breede River.

Trouble is, work is always so much more difficult to face on Monday morning.

Phone Pat Busch at (023) 626-2033.

Sunday Times, November 10, 1996

Stroll into prehistory on Robberg

The pavement is millions of years old

Seal Mountain is an unusual name for a promontory, but then the Robberg near Plettenberg Bay is an unusual place.

This rocky peninsula, reaching a height of 148 metres, stretches about four kilometres into an often-wild Indian Ocean.

The headland is a unique nature and marine reserve and has a lot to interest everyone from the amateur botanist to the professional archeologist – not to mention plain old birdwatchers and hikers.

The trail has been well laid out by Cape Nature Conservation and one of the pamphlets on the area is thought provoking. It encourages you to see this beautiful coastline in a different light.

Imagine a time, it says, when the Robberg peninsula was a hill, so far inland that you could not see the coast, and overlooked a vast plain on which giant buffalo, springbok and zebra grazed . . .

This is the scenario pieced together from the findings of archeological excavations in the 1960s and 1970s by Ray Inskip and Richard Klein.

They have shown that Nelson Bay Cave, near the base of the peninsula, was inhabited for more than 100 000 years by Stone Age people, the ancestors of the Khoi people (Hottentots and Bushmen).

The last inhabitants of the cave were probably the same folk who traded with the Portuguese survivors of the wreck of the *Saõ Gonçalo* at Plettenberg Bay in 1630.

On the north side of the peninsula near The Gap is a fascinating educational signboard identifying the different strata of rock that are visible at the side of the path. Most intriguing is a layer of conglomerate – water-worn cobbles set in sandstone. This means that at a time when the buffalo were not roaming there, this section, high up on the Robberg, was a beach. Time changes everything. Even mountains.

This conglomerate is everywhere, even forming part of the path. You could not be blamed for thinking that the authorities had mixed cobblestones with cement to make your way easier. But the pavement was made millions of summers ago.

In hiking around the Robberg, you have three circular options, each an extension of the one before. The circuit returning from The Gap will take thirty minutes. If you turn back at Witsand, allow two hours. Doing the whole route to the point will take three hours with occasional stops.

There is much to see. Whales and dolphins, seashells and oyster-catchers. Candlewood and milk-wood. The sea, the sky and the mountains meet in contrasting shades of blue. Robberg is a spectacular display of relatively un-spoilt nature. Try hard to keep it that way.

Be sure to take water to drink and avoid high tide. At the start, visit the information centre with its fascinating displays of stone-age tools and other items.

One last word: if you suffer badly from vertigo, stay at home. Although the ancient pavement slabs are wide, the gutter is a long way down in places.

Sunday Times, April 28, 1996

The Trans-Karoo Trail

In the footsteps
of the dinosaurs

Who said the Karoo was flat? The Trans-Karoo Trail near Noupoort will surprise you, for flat it is not.

Noupoort is close to Middelburg and equidistant from Cape Town, Johannesburg and Durban. Which I guess is why they call it Middelburg.

Elmarie van der Merwe and her husband opened this trail on their 10 000 hectare farm a couple of years ago. More than a thousand people already have enjoyed this rather unusual and lovingly laid-out trail.

Our group did it a few weeks back and travelled there and back on the Trans-Karoo express – a thirteen-hour journey that is fun. One can enjoy the spectacular Hex River Valley while having a meal in the comfort of the dining car. Where else can you get a sirloin steak for R18,00 and line fish and chips for R13,00?

Out in the back of beyond, the air is fresh and the night sky astonishingly clear. The silence is absolute. In other parts of the country one might reminisce about how lion and elephant used to roam there. Here, dinosaurs spring to mind.

When Africa was still part of the super-continent of Gondwanaland, this area was a vast inland sea, a terrestrial swamp.

I, who have only a passing interest in geology, found myself taking more photographs of rocks than of people as we walked through a fascinating geological zone. It shows clear evidence of a catastrophic event 250 million years ago when ninety per cent of all life on the planet was wiped out. It has been described by Professor Chris Hartnady of the University of Cape Town as "the mother of all mass extinctions". If you know what to look for on this trail, you can see the history of the Earth and life on it.

We found fascinating fingers of dolerite rock protruding straight out from cliff faces.

The trail takes three days. There is a two-day option, but if you're going to travel 750 km from Cape Town, then you might as well go for full value. The walks are twelve kilometres (four hours), nineteen kilometres (six hours) and eight kilometres (three hours).

In contrast to the fascinating

geology, the bird life and flora were disappointing. The fauna, however, is nocturnal and we saw large anteater holes and lynx spoor.

The terrain is varied with the trail passing up kloofs and dry river beds, along the edge of a sheer cliff and down into a deep valley. It's far from what you would expect of the Karoo.

The climate is extreme, so go prepared for both the Equator and the Antarctic.

Hikers are accommodated in two farmhouses and a converted barn which dates back to 1853.

For details, phone Van der Merwe at (04924) 2-2112. For a small extra charge, she will ferry your bags for you between overnight stops. For more than that you couldn't ask.

Sunday Times, November 3, 1996

Barrydale kaleidoscope

The Poor Man's
Fish River Canyon

The Fish River Canyon is closer to Cape Town than you think – and you don't need a passport to get to Barrydale to explore it.

The canyon takes only five hours instead of five days to traverse, so one could call it the Poor Man's Fish River Canyon as the similarities between them are striking – even down to the hot-water spring to soak your aching muscles in at the end.

Barrydale, east of Montagu, is on the edge of the Little Karoo, on the so-called "Inner" Garden Route, and just $2^1/_2$ hours' drive from Cape Town.

The route through the canyon is one of five trails in the area. It doesn't have a name, mainly because no one knows about it. According to Gerry Welz, who is one of life's characters and who first explored it barefoot in 1941: "Probably only fifty people have been through this canyon."

It is not as steep, wide or long as the Fish River Canyon, but it is every bit as eerie and enchanting.

The memory of soaking after the trail in hot-water springs while pouring ice-cold beer down the hatch makes me want to do it all over again.

However, don't go there thinking that breaking new ground and taking to the waters are the only attractions Barrydale has to offer.

The new owners of the Barrydale Country Inn will take you on other trails. Don't be surprised that they are English-speaking folk from Fish Hoek.

The hotel was established a hundred years ago by a Jewish trader known as O'Bromewitz.

Only being told that the founder was a McKaplan from County Cork would surprise me more.

What might surprise visitors is the colourful Amazon parrot in the pub. "Doppies", his vocabulary clearly influenced by many years of overhearing bar-room conversations, speaks fluent Afrikaans.

On our second day at the Barrydale Country Inn, the young owners obligingly took us on the Moerasrivier (Marsh River) Trail, a $4^1/_2$-hour circular route to a magnificent waterfall, reached through the most stunning array of fynbos to be seen anywhere.

The Moerasrivier Trail was es-

tablished two years ago by local legend Ben Moodie, then a ripe 84 years old. It must have something to do with the water.

The hike was entirely different from that of the day before – but that's Barrydale. The landscape ranges from harsh Karoo to lush green vineyards and montane forests, with icy waterfalls to hot springs.

The kaleidoscope of Barrydale will continue to unfold this coming summer when Gerry Welz takes us on an adventure through the kloofs of the nearby Tradouw Pass.

Place names like The Last Waterfall God Made and The Emperor's Pool make the Gatbos a place you must visit.

Break out this weekend and call the Barrydale Country Inn on (028) 572-1226 and ask Kathy for more information.

Sunday Times, May 26, 1996

The Arangieskop Trail

The mother and father
of Western Cape trails

Despite being born as recently as March 1992, this is the mother and father of all trails in the Western Cape. It is destined to become to the Western Cape what the Otter Trail is to South Africa – the prince of trails. But like the Otter Trail, it is neither for the faint of heart, nor for the weak of limb. There are many words to describe this two-day endurance test, but I'll settle for spectacular.

The distances are relatively short, as two-day trails go (9,5 km and 11,4 km), but the 9,5 km of the first day must be the longest 9,5 km in the Western Cape; nonetheless worth every gruelling step of the way. The bizarre rock formations and distorted cliff faces, the views and the virgin fynbos make the punishing climb well worthwhile. And the cherry on the top is the overnight hut at the end of it.

The second day is even more breathtaking. If you think it's all downhill just because you're on top of the mountain, think again! There is a most remarkable descent on a path which zigzags its way down a steep and narrow L-shaped gorge ending in a blind alley, out of which you have to climb. But not before you have cooled off in a picturesque swimming hole surrounded by shady butterspoon trees, among the largest I have ever seen. The tree takes its name from the growing tip of each branch bearing a remarkable resemblance to a butter spoon. In autumn you will be treated to a sensational display of red nerina – bright red spots everywhere you look. This indigenous flower is also known rather fraudulently as the Guernsey Lily. Sometime during the last century red nerina bulbs were taken from the Western Cape to Guernsey in the Channel Islands, and grown very successfully there. They were subsequently exported from Guernsey to all corners of the earth and became known as Guernsey lilies.

Drive your car to the Dassieshoek Hut in a most idyllic setting just outside Robertson, and spend the night there prior to your hike. The reward for your first day's tough climb is the Arangieskop Hut, a most pleasant surprise, and perhaps the best-equipped and well-placed mountain hut in the Cape.

Built into the rock face, this gem of a mountain retreat has, apart from a superb view over the Koo Valley, a hot shower, flush toilets, solar battery-powered electric lights, a luxurious fireplace in the centre of a delightfully rustic lounge, and upstairs bedrooms with a view. What more could you ask for? Well, there are even four double beds!

Next morning look down over the rest of the world from Arangieskop itself, as enjoyed in the 1950s by Oubaas Stevie Arangies. This peak appears on survey maps as Dassieshoek Peak, but Robertsoners know it only as Arangieskop. Mr H M O Arangies was a much-loved and respected school teacher in the postwar years and his "thing" was to climb to this highest point in the district once every couple of weeks, in the days when there was no path. Once at the top, he would flash a mirror at the dorp to let his pupils and the townsfolk know that he had arrived safely. Older locals will tell you he left Robertson at eight am and reached the top by noon. So are all legends coloured with the passage of time.

If you can do this one, the Everest of Western Cape trails, you can do all of them. But be warned, it is only for the fit and regular hiker. Like all things difficult to achieve, this one has its exceptional rewards, not least of which are two of the finest overnight huts in the Western Cape and the challenge you will find difficult to ignore.

Permits are obtainable from Robertson Municipality by phoning (023) 626-3112.

Cape Times, January 22, 1994

De Hoop Nature Reserve Part 1

A charming necklace of nature

If you haven't yet been to the southernmost tip of Africa, it's high time you went.

You'll need a whole weekend, but this is no ordinary weekend. It's primarily one for twitchers (intense birdwatchers who keep score). But there's much, much more than just birds.

At the right time of year, you can see flowers that grow nowhere else in the world. And you can see more whales with one sweep of the eye than you might ever hope to see in your entire life. Not to mention the rare Cape vulture, in comparison to which the bontebok and fish eagle (the "voice of Africa") almost pale into insignificance.

This is not the usual two-day hike. Rather, it is a series of bits and pieces, strung together in a charming necklace of nature. There is a choice of long or short trails, depending on how your fancy takes you or your particular interest, be it birds, rare plants, pottering in rock pools, or whatever. And the accommodation, apart from being more than adequate, is very reasonably priced.

As there is so much to see and do at the De Hoop Nature Reserve near Bredasdorp, let's break it up into three weekly columns covering first the vlei, next week the coast and the week after, the Potberg.

Getting there from Cape Town should take about $2^1/_2$ hours via the N2 to Caledon, there turning off to Bredasdorp. From there follow the signposts to De Hoop along 54 km of dirt road, but make sure you fill up with petrol in Bredasdorp, as you are likely to travel another 170 km before returning, with no garage along the way. Also plan to get to De Hoop before six pm when they close the gates. The prospect of running out of petrol and being locked out doesn't bear thinking about.

The vlei trail will take three to four hours and for full-on twitchers the bird life here will make even the Transvalers envious both night and day.

And then there are the herds of bontebok, eland and zebra, with the occasional reebok and ostrich pair.

If you don't fancy being trampled by a herd of stampeding

eland, you can always opt for the car trail. Yes, *car* trail! This is planned for the near future and will be an eleven-kilometre carefully laid-out route with regular observation stops, where your free guide booklet will point out plants, trees and animals of interest in that area.

The bungalows are cottagey and sort of nouveau Cape Dutch. They're well-equipped with beds and mattresses, fridge, hotplate and electric lights. Braai grids and wood are provided but must be ordered at the time of booking. To book call (028) 542-1126.

Cape Times, June 18, 1994

De Hoop Nature Reserve Part 2

A whale of a time

If you haven't seen a whale breaching then you haven't experienced the truly *awesome* sight of the planet's largest animal just having a *jol*. At De Hoop Nature Reserve near the southernmost tip of our continent, you will see between May and November more whales with one sweep of the eye than you might have seen in your entire life. This is the southern right whale; so called rather sadly, because they were the "right" whales to kill.

They have longer and more flexible baleen (food filters), which were once valuable to industry. Also their carcasses floated and were easy to tow and strip at sea. For these so-called attributes, they were hunted almost to extinction.

Most of the southern right adults you will see at De Hoop are each probably the size of ten elephants. When that weight hits the water in a breach (when they jump almost clear of the water and come crashing down on their sides) it is really something to see. With creatures up to eighteen metres long (the height of a six-storey building) and weighing 45 tons, this is a sight never to be forgotten. Occasionally you might hear the sound of a huge hollow metal tank bumping against the rocks. It is not what it seems. What you are hearing is the trumpeting of a whale. It's eerie and yet strangely beautiful. You are hearing something very special. The conservation officer in charge refers rather irreverently to this experience as an "ecogasm".

August to October are the best months for whale-watching, when there are likely to be in excess of a hundred individuals in the area. You are bound to see whales, for this bay (uncomfortably close to what used to be a missile testing range) is the maternity and nursery area where the females come all the way from 55 degrees south latitude to calve. There is a supposition that the cows don't feed at all during this time, and, although suckling their calves, still manage to live off fat reserves for up to three months. Very few bulls are found in the nursery area.

But whales are not the only reason you need to do the coastal trail of De Hoop. Explore the endless crystal-clear rock pools with their colourful water gardens, and stumble across the occasional Khoikhoi

(Hottentot) midden – perlemoen and limpet shells indicating a human presence of long, long ago. A word of warning though: footwear should be suitable for getting wet while at the same time offering protection against sharp rocks. On no account be tempted to stand on the thin platforms jutting out from the cliffs and coastline. By virtue of their limestone composition they are fragile, and the cost of a helicopter rescue could ruin your entire day. Notice the African black oystercatcher, a completely black bird except for bright red legs, bill and eyes. Despite its being the second rarest endemic breeding bird in South Africa, you are bound to see a good few here.

The De Hoop Coastal Trail is reached by driving fourteen kilometres from your well-equipped cottages at De Hoop (see last week's column) to Koppie Alleen, from where the route follows the coast, meandering between tidal pools, outcrops and beaches for six kilometres, before returning along a Jeep track just 100 metres inland.

To book the De Hoop cottages, call (028) 542-1126.

Cape Times, June 25, 1994

De Hoop Nature Reserve Part 3

Cape vultures – nature's refuse collectors

Last week whales and this week vultures – all in the fascinating De Hoop Nature Reserve some fifty kilometres beyond Bredasdorp. This weekend getaway will see you comfortably settled in well-appointed cottages, from which you can do short hikes, bird-watching alongside the vlei or whale-watching on the coast.

A third possibility is to climb the Potberg, 26 km from your cottage in the northeastern part of the reserve. This small mountain (611 metres) is a sandstone island in a sea of shale and limestone. This explains why certain plant species are endemic to this little mountain and grow nowhere else in the world – not even one kilometre away. They are as captive as a crawling insect on a remote South Sea island.

At least ten such unique species exist here, including the beautiful, deep red *Protea denticulata*, named after the denticles, or tiny teeth, on its leaf surfaces. It blooms from mid-August until the end of October.

A large sandstone building at the base of the Potberg was built by Anders Ohlsson of brewery fame, but has been converted into an en-vironmental education centre to accommodate large parties from schools and other groups. The Klipspringer Trail starts here and presents the hiker with the best opportunity of seeing the rare Cape vulture. A side trip to the peak is well worth the effort.

Most people have a negative image of vultures with their long, bare necks and hunched shoulders just sitting around and waiting for death so they can feed on another creature's misfortune. The squabbling and bloody mess at the scene of the carcass is not a pretty sight either. And yet vultures fill a vital ecological role by cleansing the veld of rotting carcasses that would otherwise spread disease. They are in fact nature's refuse collection team, helping the farmer to keep his stock healthy.

It comes as a surprise therefore to learn that some farmers in the past have shot or poisoned them on the pretext that they kill lambs. This is nonsense, as their feet are clearly designed for standing and not for catching prey. They are scavengers, not birds of prey.

With a wingspan of 2,5 metres

and weighing around eight kilograms, the Cape vulture is a joy to behold in flight. These huge birds regularly fly 200 km a day in their search for carrion and can reach enormous heights. The world altitude record is held by a closely-related Ruppel's griffin vulture flying at 11 500 metres.

How they can survive the very subzero temperatures at that height is a wonder of nature. And with a naked neck *nogal*.

The reason their scrawny neck is bare of feathers is that they often stick their heads right into a carcass to feed on entrails. A feathered neck would soon become dirty and bacteriologically undesirable. Think of it as a surgical glove. Isn't nature amaaaazing?

To book this string of pearls, phone the De Hoop Nature Reserve at (028) 542-1126. If all the cottages are booked for the popular spring flowers and whale-watching of August to October, then consider roughing it at the camp site which is almost sure to have space.

The flower power will get you through any discomfort on the hard ground. Alternatively, arrange accommodation in Arniston and enter the reserve as a day visitor.

Cape Times, July 2, 1994

Warmwaterberg Hot Springs and Trail

And Ronnie's Sex Shop

The magic of the hot water. That's what this trail is all about. Just on the other side of Barrydale, in the Little Karoo, is Warmwaterberg – a hot-spring holiday getaway that has real charm. Lying in a hot swimming pool deep into the night, under a new moon, you will never ever see the Milky Way this way again. The warmth. The startling clarity. And the utter peace.

A current advertisement for a BMW convertible says it all; ". . . and you thought the Sistine Chapel had a beautiful ceiling".

However, it also has a downside. There is not a single cold tap in this delightful olde-worlde resort.

You can have any water you like as long as it's hot. And that includes the loo. Don't whatever you do flush while in the seated position. You could get really steamed up about it. Condensation on the family jewels is not fun. Ask me. I know.

This delightful spot is a three-hour drive from Cape Town, along the Worcester-Robertson-Montagu road to a point 26 km beyond Barrydale. You'll know when you're there, because in the middle of absolutely nowhere is this sex shop at the side of the road. At least, that's what it says on the building: "Ronnie's Sex Shop".

Ronnie is a local English-speaking bachelor farmer (rare in these parts). One could not be blamed for thinking his only wish was to "spread a little happiness by the body" or that maybe he got caught with his fingers in the cookie jar, so to speak. But the truth is a bunch of his friends visiting from further afield added the extra word after a night of revelry. "Ronnie's Shop" was orginally a roadside farm stall. Now it's a landmark in the conservative Karoo.

Right opposite the sex shop is Warmwaterberg, which boasts more than peace and tranquillity, blue mountains and red sunsets. It also has a hiking trail, which, although only 5,5 km long, is just right for this lazy place. It takes in koppies, ravines, and flats without ever threatening hard work. And then there's always the hot baths in which to soak afterwards. I've always found hot-water springs to be somewhat debilitating, causing this party animal to fade rather quickly.

Strangely, I found, this was not the case here. And you can even drink the water without that unpleasant sulphur smell.

Accommodation is in a characterful old building of many rooms, with all mod cons provided, except food. At R43 per person per night on weekends and R38 on weekdays, you can't get much better than that. The farm has been in the hands of the Le Grange family for more than a hundred years. Bookings can be made by calling Barrydale (028) 572-1609.

Take to the therapeutic waters of Warmwaterberg this weekend and soak up the solid white cloud of the Milky Way.

Lourdes, eat your heart out.

Cape Times, August 13, 1994

The Klapperbos and Elandsberg Trails

Stanley's Light and wrap-around spectacular

Ladysmith with a "y" is in Kwa-Zulu Natal but Ladismith (with an "i") is only about $3^{1}/_{2}$ hours drive from Cape Town along the Inner Garden route, via Worcester, Robertson and Montague. If you approach it by night you are bound to see *Stanley se liggie* (Stanley's Light) high up on the mountainside above the town. Take careful note, because this is the height to which you will climb on the strenuous Elandsberg Trail. Provided you are fit, don't let the strenuous bit put you off. A member of our party coined the phrase "wrap-around spectacular". That just about sums it up.

Stanley's Light, to which you climb, must make Ladismith unique among Platteland towns. Residents claim it is a tourist attraction and if for any reason it stops working, the townsfolk feel uncomfortable and immediately summon Stanley's successor to rectify the situation.

Stanley de Wit, now 68, placed the light there in 1963 on the second anniversary of Republic Day. Over the next thirty years, he climbed the mountain 271 times to maintain his light which was powered by a bicycle dynamo driven by a water wheel. It burns 24 hours a day all year round. In 1993, however, the dynamo was replaced with an alternator and a sealed-beam car lamp. And so was Oom Stanley – by a younger man. But the name lingers on and the light continues to welcome residents home.

The trail leading to it is one of two day hikes the town has to offer. The Elandsberg Trail is a twelve-kilometre/six-hour circular route with some pretty steep sections; whereas the Klapperbos Trail, just four kilometres before the town, is a far less strenuous 12,6-km/four-hour circular route, over relatively easy terrain.

The majestic Towerkop, with its split peak, looms above both trails. Legend has it that an angry witch struck the peak with her wand, causing the very obvious cleavage, which can be seen from a great distance.

It even forms the trademark of the local well-known brand of cheese.

The difference in vegetation between the two trails just seven kilometres apart is remarkable. The

Elandsberg Trail is typical montane fynbos including *Protea aristata*. Although not rare, this protea with leaves like pine needles is confined exclusively to this, the Kleinswartberg mountain range. Only known to the general public since 1960, it has become one of South Africa's best-known proteas.

The Klapperbos Trail, on the other hand, sports succulent shrubs of the arid Klein Karoo region. Why the trail should be named after the klapperbos (Chinese lantern) is quite beyond me. It seems that the resident herds of eland made a long-since-finished meal of them, for there was not one to be seen. Karoo spekboom, on the other hand, with its bright green, succulent, stubby leaves, is everywhere.

Accommodation is available at various places in the town, including two hotels and guesthouses, or, as our party did, you can stay at Warmwaterberg Hot Springs, fifty kilometres on the Cape Town side of Ladismith. (See page 188.)

To book the Elandsberg Trail, call Cape Nature Conservation on (028) 551-1077 and for the Klapperbos Trail the Ladismith Municipality on (028) 551-1023.

Cape Times, August 27, 1994

Cederberg Part 1

The Great Sculptor's own art gallery

The Cederberg has a special magic all of its own. Ask anyone who's been there. It is the Great Sculptor's own art gallery, where He has on display some truly amazing shapes and forms.

It's certainly different from any other mountain range in South Africa and only $2^{1}/_{2}$ hours drive from Cape Town. Get there via Malmesbury, Piketberg and Citrusdal, turning off the N7 to Algeria. Not the one in North Africa. This Algeria is only eighteen kilometres along a dirt road deep into the Cederberg. The French forester who was appointed superintendent of forests for the Cape Colony in 1880, Count de Regne, visited this area in 1882 and was so struck by its likeness to the Atlas Mountains of North Africa that he suggested the name Algeria for the proposed forest station.

The area is particularly rich in Bushman paintings, especially in the north where caves are plentiful and rock formations at their most bizarre. Leopards roam freely and there were said to be as many as forty individuals counted in a recent survey. The cedars, after which the range is named, are alas an endangered species because of gross exploitation during the nineteenth century. Rather strangely Cederberg is the correct spelling rather than Cedarberg. The National Place Names Committee ruled it that way, presumably as a compromise between the English Cedarberg and the Afrikaans Sederberg.

You can have the Cederberg as a casual day walk alongside a babbling brook or as a week-long megamarathon. You call the tune. A weekend trail is probably a happy compromise and a number of possibilities present themselves. The walk to Crystal Pool and back is pretty strenuous but highly rewarding. But don't expect comfortable huts with bunks and mattresses as supplied by Cape Nature Conservation. This is a wilderness area and as such a rough shelter is about the best you can expect.

This trek of 36 km over rugged terrain presents a good cross section of the real Cederberg magic. The route starts at Algeria Forest Station and climbs steeply to the Middelberg Huts. On the way up

you will zigzag through a sparse forest of cedars. Savour them, for there are very few left. They bear a remarkable resemblance to the cypress, to which they are related.

Cedars are extremely slow growers and under ideal conditions will only reach a trunk diameter of 60 cm in 150 years. On less suitable sites, growth is much slower. The Clanwilliam cedar is limited to a narrow 50-km-long strip in a narrow altitude range and is further confined almost exclusively to rocky terrain, which affords good protection from its greatest predator – fire. It is particularly susceptible to fire because of its highly aromatic resin.

But alas, despite the natural protection of rocky terrain, fire gets to most of these trees in the end. Yet cedars were the dominant species in these mountains, probably for many thousands of years. So what happened to change all this so suddenly? In a couple of words – man

arrived. Or more to the point, the white man. Forestry records show that of the eighty fires recorded in the Cederberg this century, six were caused by lightning, four by rock falls and ten from unknown causes. The remaining sixty were directly attributed to human folly.

A highlight of the first day's walk is Cathedral Rocks, a wonderful example of Mother Nature's talents. Crystal Pool itself is, in fact, three or four small pools in a protected and really beautiful amphitheatre.

During good weather it is best to find a good spot to sleep under the stars near the pools, as the hut is very far from water. One thing you can be sure of though – you are being watched by leopards. This is, after all, the real wilderness.

Bookings and permits from Cederberg Wilderness Area. Call (027) 482-2812.

Cape Times, October 1, 1994

Cederberg Part 2

Snow proteas and leopard traps

From the top of Sneeuberg Peak (2 027 metres) on a clear day, not only can you see the entire Cederberg range, but even Table Mountain. Getting up there is another story – very easy for rock climbers, but perhaps a little hair-raising for some casual hikers. But nobody says you have to climb to the top of the highest peak in the Cederberg. There are far too many other things of interest along the way, which make the macho bit unimportant.

The start of the Sneeuberg adventure is at Eikeboom, 237 km from Cape Town, reached via Malmesbury and Piketberg. Eikeboom is seventeen kilometres beyond the Algeria Forest Station in the heart of Cederberg country, where huge rocks are strewn about like toys thrown out of the child's cot.

Leave your car under the old oaks at Eikeboom and follow the Jeep track up Sederhoutkloof. Nowadays there's hardly a cedar to be seen, but there is plenty of waboom (wagon tree). The wood from these indigenous proteas was used in the old days as felloes (rims) for wagon wheels, due to its hardness. Some fifteen minutes after starting you will notice an old leopard trap. It is probably 150 years old, and dates back to when the area was farmed.

The Cederberg Wilderness Area is probably one of the few areas in the Cape where leopard still roam freely. They are opportunistic feeders that prey on a wide range of animals, including large herbivores more than twice their weight, as well as carrion.

In this area, dassies are by far the most abundant prey species, followed by klipspringer and grey reebok. However, their catholic taste has resulted in regular incidents of stock raiding, which hasn't made local farmers too happy.

After the leopard trap, the Jeep track begins climbing steeply, the waboom get bigger, and the baboon sentries warn the troop of your presence. A couple of hours should see you to the hut, where you can decide if you are intent on conquering the Cederberg's highest peak or are content to stroll to the Maltese Cross and back.

Our party took the macho option, and encountered two remarkable

things. The first was a number of snow protea (*P. cryophila*) still in flower in mid-April. This rare and beautiful plant occurs only above the snow line on the highest peaks in the Cederberg and nowhere else in the world. The other surprise was to see Elsie Esterhuysen, South Africa's most distinguished contemporary botanical collector, descending from the peak with the determination and sure-footedness of a mountain goat. Elsie is an internationally acclaimed collector of high-altitude plant material. But what was so remarkable about seeing her coming down Sneeuberg Peak like an express train? It was her eightieth birthday.

Day two of this hike reveals the truly awesome sight of Duiwelsgat and the trail ends at a most beautiful swimming hole just a couple of minutes from your waiting second car.

For permits call the Cederberg Wilderness Area Booking Officer on (027) 482-2812.

Cape Times, October 8, 1994

Cederberg Part 3

The Cracks and the Cross

The Cracks and the Cross – my all-time favourites. This is Cederberg magic at its very best. The Wolfberg Cracks can be explored in one day (throw in the Wolfberg Arch as an optional extra if you feel up to it), and the Maltese Cross the next day. These amazing rock formations will blow your mind, especially if you've never been to the Cederberg before.

Just the drive there and back is worth it, even if you don't hike. Get there from Cape Town via Malmesbury and Citrusdal to Algeria Forest Station. Twenty-nine kilometres beyond Algeria is Dwarsrivier Farm, your starting point for both the Wolfberg Cracks and the Maltese Cross.

For an interesting variation return to Cape Town via Op die Berg and the Koue Bokkeveld, Prince Alfred's Hamlet, Ceres, Bain's Kloof, Wellington and Agter Paarl, but make sure you fill up with petrol outside Citrusdal.

There are numerous farms in the area offering accommodation and you must obtain a permit from one of them, for most of the hike is on private land. For this purpose phone Mrs H Nieuwoudt of the farm Dwarsrivier (027) 482-2825. Also check when they can arrange a wine tasting. Despite the extremes of climate, they produce some very palatable wines in the Cederberg. Here I am reminded of one of my favourite wine quotations by Thiophile Malvezine (whoever he may be):

Wine is made to be drunk
As women are to be loved.
Profit by the freshness of youth
Or the splendour of maturity;
Do not await decrepitude.

But back to the subject matter. The Maltese Cross is a sight you will not easily forget. It stands roughly the equivalent of a six-storey building on a flat plain, begging the question of how on earth it got there. The truth is it's been there for hundreds of millions of years. Over that time the land and rock around it slowly eroded away, leaving behind this amazing monolith.

The Wolfberg Cracks (two of them) are an incredible experience, if you can force your way through the second crack – not for the oversized or unfit. The faint of heart

should take the first crack alternative – big enough through which to drive a double-decker bus. But the more adventurous simply must not miss one of the Cederberg's priceless gems, the second crack. Simply awesome.

A side excursion from your bungalow could be a trip to Stadsaal. A series of open caves, it is said to have been the inaugural meeting place of the National Party in 1919. Graffiti on the walls include the name of D F Malan. Much older indications of a bygone era are only a few metres away in the form of San (Bushman) paintings, depicting the time elephant roamed freely here.

The San inhabited this region from at least 100 000 years ago.

Essentially a religious art, their paintings record the power and experience of the medicine men. They gained their "power" by going into trances induced by rhythmic dancing, clapping and singing. After coming out of their dreamlike state they would paint what they had seen, and their visions often included animals that were important in their beliefs and folklore.

The eland is the most commonly painted animal and the bodies almost always tend to be elongated and small, as the feeling of being stretched out and tiny is an hallucination commonly experienced during a trance.

The weird and wonderful rock formations that will captivate you in the Cederberg are no hallucinations. They are very real, and just waiting to be seen for the first time.

Cape Times, October 15, 1994

Boosmansbos Wilderness Area

"Angry man" belies the serenity of this place

Remember Walt Disney's *Magic Forest*? Well, it simply has to have been filmed right here in the Western Cape. You could not be blamed for expecting to see Peter Pan and Tinker Bell, Snow White and the Seven Dwarfs or Bambi and many others. I'm sure they're all in this densely and diversely wooded indigenous forest, just a few kilometres north of Heidelberg.

Sylvan beauty such as this simply doesn't deserve a name as harsh as *Boosmansbos*. *Boosman* note. Not *Boesman*. A boosman is an angry man, which somehow seems highly inappropriate in the soothing atmosphere of this forest of many parts. Cypress, milkwood, yellowwood, candlewood, red and white alder and much much more. At one place there is a huge stinkwood actually straddling the river. Two huge roots one metre in diameter form an A-frame over the river with one root going into each bank. The apex is all of six metres above the water. Which means that when this giant was a seedling, the surrounding land was six metres higher than it is now.

It's difficult to imagine how I overlooked this gem for as long as I did. It has what is arguably the most breathtakingly beautiful mountain scenery in the Cape. Some say in the country. And if any two-day 27-km hike can be described as non-strenuous, this can.

But don't expect too much from the overnight accommodation. No beds or mattresses or furniture of any kind. Just four stone walls and a tin roof. There are two huts at Helderfontein and it's Hobson's Choice. You can either have the one with the gaping wooden floor or – if you don't fancy a draught up the shaft – you can have the one with the very solid and equally cold concrete floor. *Freeze* your butt off instead.

However, on the positive side they are perfectly waterproof, as I discovered with some relief one foul and stormy night. But this is, after all, a Wilderness Area, which according to the Forest Act of 1984 is: "An undeveloped area, uninhabited by man. It should retain an intrinsically wild appearance and give visitors a feeling of isolation from the outside world." That it

does in no small measure. So if you're not sincere about getting back to your roots, stay at home and watch TV. (Not preaching – I take that option myself sometimes.)

The first day (six hours/fourteen kilometres) is pleasant with rolling green hills and deep wooded kloofs. The ascent is gentle and consistent. But nothing can prepare you for the sheer rugged beauty of day two. And that's in spite of the fact that seventy per cent of it is down a gravel road. It's known as the Barend Koen Road, in the very best South African tradition of naming everything after somebody. This dude was the foreman in charge of construction in 1942. I mean *really*. I ask you with tears in my eyes. Why not Winston Churchill Way or Adolf Hitler Highway or Oubaas Smuts Street? But Barend *who*? To add insult to injury, the road leads to nowhere. It was built to make the area more accessible for afforestation, but shortly after it was completed, the wilderness concept came into vogue. Thank goodness. You might only have been looking at pines and gums instead of all this.

Permits are obtainable from Cape Nature Conservation on the Heidelberg exchange (029) 342-2412. A good idea is to spend the Friday night on the doorstep to the trail, to get an early start. Accommodation is available at Honeywood Guest Cottages, by calling General G D Moodie or his son John on (029) 342-1839. General Moodie is the retired head of the army and by all reports a charming host. General Moodie's ancestor Benjamin Moodie, the tenth Laird of Melsetter in the Orkneys, emigrated here from Scotland in 1817, bringing at his own expense some 200 settlers, mostly Scottish. The immigration scheme regrettably did not succeed, but the area became the Moodie family home for many generations. For the less demanding, camping sites are available at the start of the trail.

Cape Times, October 22, 1994

HEY-HO. HEY-HO

Jubilee Creek Walk

The ghosts of Boomtown

If you're in Cape Town, Knysna seems like an awfully long way to drive to do a couple of hours' walk in paradise. But then paradise doesn't come easily. Mainly you just wait until you are in the area. But don't wait too long.

Jubilee Creek just reeks with history.

The heady stuff of the Knysna gold rush. And the sound of birdsong piercing the silence of a deep green indigenous forest.

Only the really old yellowwoods and stinkwoods can remember the diggers. They poured in from California, Australia and Cornwall, shortly after local farmer James Hooper discovered a gold nugget in the nearby Karatara River. And that was in 1876 – some years before the birth of Johannesburg. Gold fever, let's make no mistake about it, was conceived in Knysna and only born in Joey's.

Get there by taking the Rheenendal turnoff, at the top of the hill, some seven kilometres on the Cape Town side of Knysna. About twenty kilometres off the N2 is heaven.

Jubilee Creek is a lawned clearing in a dense indigenous forest, bisected by Millwood Creek.

And birdsong.

The trail follows the river bank for 45 minutes before finishing up at an idyllic pool and waterfall. And just to add some spice, right next to the pool is yet another mineshaft. (You could not have missed seeing three others along the way.)

Don't enter the old mineshafts without a torch; in any event, do so with caution.

The short-lived boom of the Knysna gold rush centred on nearby Millwood.

In 1887 the tented village turned into a full-on town almost overnight. Apart from the 600 diggers, there were another 400 hangers-on. Like the local publican and gunsmith for instance. Around every sun there are satellites – or are they not perhaps parasites? The daisy chain of business is not always pretty.

Millwood in its heyday was made up of 75 buildings plus six hotels. The Commercial, Central, Pioneer, Howell's, Holt's Temperance and the Millwood each had a

tale to tell. The ubiquitous Royal and the Masonic were conspicuous by their absence. There was also a Standard Bank, a post office and – wait for it – a music hall. A bordello was probably part of the scene as well, except no-one talked about it. A digger had to have his fun, after all is said and done.

The mine shafts you will see on this walk are just the tip of the iceberg. Apart from many enthusiastic shafts sunk to extract the yellow metal from the ground, a fair bit was alluvial gold, taken from the creek.

The collapse of the Millwood Goldfields was as dramatic as its conception. In 1888 it started going downhill and within a couple of years the diggers felt the lure of the newly established goldfields on the Witwatersrand. Millwood and Jubilee Creek quietly lay down and died. Its shacks were dismantled and relocated. All that remains are a couple of buildings used by hikers on the Outeniqua Trail as an overnight stop. But omnipresent is the ghost of an abandoned mining town. If you listen carefully, you will hear the picks and the excitement of a century ago.

This is a one-way walk, returning by the same route. But don't let that put you off. It's pristine indigenous forest with absolutely no uphill and the bonus of a swim at the terminus. So much for so little effort.

Cape Times, October 29, 1994

The Greyton-McGregor Trail

Fresh leopard tracks

Anyone who knows hiking in the Western Cape knows the Greyton-McGregor Trail. Very few know it as the Boesmanskloof Trail – its official name. It joins the towns of Greyton and McGregor by means of a delightful hiking route only fourteen kilometres long.

However, if you choose to leave a car at each end, to avoid a double walk back to the start, you will need to travel not fourteen, but 280 km by road. Much easier to walk back. And, anyway, we've had many a good party at the Greyton Hotel around the piano in the pub. That's what hiking is all about. Like banging your head against a brick wall. It's lovely when you stop . . .

The route was originally intended to be a mountain pass. It was begun in the depression years of the 1930s using cheap vagrant labour. (Brilliant idea – why not reintroduce it?) Starting from both ends, the road reached the high point at each end, when in 1941 work was stopped as a result of embezzlement of funds. Apart from the start and finish of the trail, which are steep, most of it is fairly level, with a waterfall swimming pool en route, which is quite one of the finest in the Western Cape mountains. The story goes that the rugby teams from Greyton and McGregor used to take turns to cross the mountains over a weekend to play one another. The visitors were obviously at a disadvantage.

Start at the McGregor end if you wish to enjoy the bright lights of Greyton, with its one-star hotel and two well-known country guest houses (Greyton Lodge and The Post House). Then there's always what we as university students used to call the Municipal Hotel – the local camping site.

Starting from Greyton, you have a choice of two places to stay at the McGregor end of the trail. Whipstock Farm and Die Galg will provide hikers with all basic needs.

In the deep valley between both ends, the rugged loneliness of the area will strike you, along with the large variety of ericas and proteas. Fresh leopard tracks and droppings are frequently reported, making the rugged loneliness even lonelier.

Roughly one third of the way

towards Greyton you will reach the highlight of the trail. This is a superb inky black pool into which drops a perennial waterfall, followed by numerous other deep pools all the way down the gorge.

The trip one way from McGregor to Greyton will take you about $5^1/_2$ hours, allowing plenty of time for a swim and lunch.

Greyton was founded in 1854 and named after the Governor of the Cape Colony, Sir George Grey. McGregor, founded a few years later in 1861, was first called Lady Grey after his memsahib. But this was later changed to McGregor after the Robertson missionary, the Rev. Andrew McGregor, presumably to avoid confusion with the town of the same name in the Eastern Cape. It was also suggested in less polite circles that the governor and his wife needed a mountain range to separate them.

To book this popular trail phone (023) 5-3621 (Vrolijkheid Nature Conservation Centre at McGregor).

Cape Times, November 19, 1994

The Montagu Trail

Classical music and malt whisky in heaven

You've just finished a long day's walk. You've had a hot shower in the mountains and you are sitting on the veranda of a stone hut.

The hut nestles in a tight and deep kloof, with cliffs towering all around. An awesome sight in the fading light of evening. Classical music plays just a little more than in the background, so that an echo follows it from the surrounding cliffs. In your hand is the very finest malt whisky that money can buy. Neat with a block of ice. This is heaven.

I am neither a lover of classical music nor malt whisky. But that's what you do in heaven. I know. I've done it.

The Klipspringer Hut on the Montagu Trail will give you this taste of paradise. Not to mention the flush toilets. In the mountains that's real luxury. Beats the hell out of a long drop, where it just doesn't seem to go away afterwards.

The Montagu Trail is a delightful weekend hike that is really two one-day trails which both start and end at the same spot, forming a distorted figure of eight, with the Klipspringer Hut in the middle.

Flowers and bird life abound on both days.

The longer and more strenuous of the two is Bloupunt, so perhaps a good idea is to do that first, on the Saturday after a Friday night's sleep-over. The Bloupunt section offers a constantly changing panorama on the way to the top of the highest peak in the area. From this point you can see no less than five towns in the area (Montagu, Ashton, Bonnievale, McGregor and Robertson).

After your first day's walk, when you have tired of the classical music and malt whisky, and darkness has settled heavily on the kloof, it is not an evil thought to bear in mind that the hot springs and ladies' bar at the Avalon Springs Hotel are a mere fifteen-minute walk, plus five-minute drive, away. Just a thought . . . Not for the purists mind you. They're probably going to throw me out of the Mountain Club now.

The Cogmanskloof on day two is a cakewalk by comparison. Only $4^1/_2$ hours, which gives you (a) plenty of time to recover from the wheels coming off at the Avalon

Springs (it's the hot water that does it) and (b) enough time to get home again to start hyperventilating about Monday.

The Cogmanskloof section reaches a height of less than half that of Bloupunt, but still offers a beautiful view of Montagu and the surrounding cliff faces. The first two kilometres are tough, but the remaining ten kilometres are easy going.

Apart from fynbos, the area also reeks of history. The Anglo-Boer War was very much a reality here, as witnessed by a nearby 1899 fortification. The name Cogmanskloof does not honour a Boer hero as one might expect, but rather unexpectedly takes its Anglicised name from the Khoikhoi (Hottentot) tribe of Koekemans.

Once on the downward slope of Cogmanskloof, you'll have time to notice the cliffs on the far side of Droogekloof, as if they had been painted bright yellow over vast areas by graffiti vandals. But fear not. This mass graffiti is the work of Mother Nature. Seldom are you likely to see such an incredible amount of yellow lichen concentrated in one area.

To book this wonderful weekend, call the Montagu Municipality on (0234) 42472.

Cape Times, December 2, 1994

The Swellendam Trail

In the Republic
of Swellendam

The third oldest town in South Africa certainly has a great deal of charm if not a fair bit of cheek to boot. Swellendam, in 1795, had the audacity to unilaterally declare itself a republic.

Named after Governor Hendrik Swellengrebel and his wife Helena Ten Damme, the town shocked the all-powerful Dutch East India Company by storming the gracious Drosdy building with armed burghers and proclaiming a republic. They declared themselves answerable only to the Batavian Republic and not the Dutch East India Company. (Only a few months earlier Napoleon had conquered the Netherlands and renamed it the Batavian Republic, no doubt giving more than a modicum of inspiration to the Swellendammers.)

Among their "Ten Articles of Demand" were complaints about inadequate education, a right to free trade, corruption of certain officials, squatters' rights and an exemption from tolls and taxes. So, in 200 years, what's changed? The Swellendam Revolution and the euphoria of independence didn't last long though – only $4^{1}/_{2}$ months

in fact, when the Cape was lost to Britain at the Battle of Muizenberg.

The charming town, apart from its other attributes, marks the beginning and end of one of the country's best trails. The Swellendam Trail is not for the uninitiated, for there are places, especially on the first day, where the top never seems to come. But the rewards are greater than the ordeal.

I had the pleasure, a year or so ago, of meeting the person who established and laid out this trail from raw bush. It wasn't a hairy macho muscular forester, but a tiny slip of a thing called Jaynee Levy. It's difficult to imagine this superfit American lass being such an accomplished mountain goat and the doyenne of South African hiking authors. The top of her head was about level with the top of my paunch. Well, not really. But she is tiny and slightly built and it's odd that we had to import someone from the USA to lay out our trails for us. The Amatola Trail in the Ciskei and others are also the result of her pioneering work.

An unusual feature of the Swel-

lendam Trail is that it presents two-, three-, four-, or even six-day options. There are no fewer than six overnight huts on the oblong circular route with short cuts making it possible to short circuit. A weekend option would be to spend the Saturday night at Boskloof hut, with its excellent swimming hole and "foefie slide", and return on the Sunday via Ten o'Clock Peak. The view from this peak is worth all the effort, with Swellendam nestling below and the Indian Ocean in the distance. On a clear day you can see the very tip of Africa.

If you start early enough up Ten o'Clock Peak, you will see cobwebs glisten in the early morning sun with the jewels of nature. Dewdrops on a freshly constructed spider's web is something that never fails to fill me with awe. Just a few hours earlier the industrious spider sets its trap by releasing a fine silk thread, which floats on the gentle air currents. With luck the sticky thread becomes attached to a twig or other object, and the foundation is laid for an ornate food trap, which despite its complexity, will take only about an hour to build. The silk is able to stretch up to 25% of its length before breaking, which is remarkable. Certain spider silk is the strongest natural fibre known.

The best time to do this trail, surprisingly, is midwinter. The driest time of the year is June and the wettest month, by a long way, is February – and I checked this with the appropriate metereological authorities. Bookings can be made through Cape Nature Conservation at (0291) 4-1410.

Cape Times, January 20, 1995

The Dassieshoek Trail

And the soul
of the ant

Isn't it special to be able to swim in water you can drink? We take this so much for granted in the Western Cape, while in most other parts of South Africa it is unsafe to *swim* in river water, let alone actually *drink* it.

The Dassieshoek Trail on the outskirts of Robertson presents a number of such opportunities to cool off, drink up and move on. But the baptism is one of fire. The first day of this two-day trail is 23 km – a fair distance in anyone's book. And the first twelve kilometres are completely without water through semi-arid Karoo scrub, not to mention uphill, under the scorching sun. But suddenly the vegetation changes from Karoo scrub to lush green mountain fynbos, as the path traverses the base of the Langeberg range, through a series of pretty kloofs.

But despite the distance (day two is fifteen kilometres) the Dassieshoek Trail is not strenuous – especially when compared to its other Robertson counterpart, the Arangieskop Trail (see page 180).

Dassieshoek accommodation gives you most of life's little luxuries. If you spend the Friday night at the beginning of the trail at the Silver Strand resort on the Breede River, you'll even get a refrigerator thrown in, along with a hot bath and electric lights. A Friday night sojourn before the trail is advisable, due to the early start you need to do the 23 km. And you also want to beat the sun on the first waterless morning before it beats you. But it's a well-built and well-designed trail, as the sun is always behind you. Just make sure you have sunscreen for the back of your legs.

At the end of the first day's trek is a converted farmhouse which sleeps (heaven forbid) 35 people in the most idyllic surroundings. As there are only two showers and two toilets, I shudder to imagine the night it is full.

Along the way you are bound to see large so-called ant hills. Rather surprisingly they're not inhabited by ants at all, but by termites (popularly known as white ants). Termites, however, are far removed from ants, and are more closely related to cockroaches. But ants are far more fascinating. There are

fourteen different species of ant commonly found in the Western Cape. They enjoy colourful common names such as the hotrod ant, droptail ant, nutcracker ant, black hag ant, red driver ant, cocktail ant, and the pugnacious ant, more commonly known (in less polite circles) as the "ball biter".

They seem to communicate mainly by signals conveyed through secretions of pheromones – hormone-like substances that stimulate various responses such as "food", "follow this trail" and "danger". Their behaviour is completely instinctive and mechanical. There is no evidence that ants are capable of learnt behaviour. They are remarkably strong for their size and can carry loads equivalent to a man picking up a ten-ton weight. These tiny creatures, and their pivotal role in the delicate balance of nature, are a constant source of fascination to me.

The second day of the Dassieshoek Trail is quite different, with the midpoint being a most pleasant swimming hole, complete with beach. As day two is only $5^1/_2$ hours long, depending on your urgency to get home, you could arrange to have breakfast, brunch or lunch here.

To book this gem that will present you with all kinds of vegetation and microclimates, phone the Robertson Municipality on (023) 626-3112.

Cape Times, February 3, 1995

The Groot Winterhoek Wilderness Area

To hell and back again

Hell is a really beautiful place. Just as long as it's in the Groot Winterhoek mountains above Porterville. Where's Porterville you say?

It's one of those places where Afrikaans is spoken with a deliciously gentle "brei". No hard rolling of the r's here. Only the gurgling French way – obviously a strong Huguenot influence. In fact you could almost find your way there by following the "brei" route – Malmesbury, Moorreesburg, Piketberg. Then right turn to Porterville.

Before you know it you're winding your way up the tortuous Dasklip Pass, before coming to the Groot Winterhoek Wilderness Area on top of the mountain. It's a major plus that you can drive your car to the top, and then just enjoy a relatively level, if somewhat long, hike to purgatory.

This is a two-day hike with a sleep in the mountains. Your sleep, if you can get it, is on a hard *misvloer* in *De Tronk* (the jail). But fear not. The spartan hut was in fact a farmhouse, not a jail.

The farm was so named because it was often cut off from the outside world by a river which flooded in winter. Incarceration was by the elements and not the authorities.

As a weekend trail, it's longer than most (twenty kilometres/ seven hours plus 21 km/$7^{1}/_{2}$ hours). However, it is strenuous only in its length, for most of it is over fairly level ground. You will probably finish with weary limbs, but you won't be out of breath. There is an abundance of water, with at least five excellent swimming places, many decorated with the most exquisite ericas and disas.

The second day of the hike presents you with the *pièce de résistance*. Die Hel is quite unforgettable. One can't help being reminded of the Big Hole in Kimberley, Except this one's much prettier and a hell of a lot older. By a few million years, come to think of it. There is an enormous seventy by fifty metre seemingly bottomless pool, surrounded on three sides by sheer cliffs and caves, with a beautiful white waterfall cascading into the inky black water.

This is a wilderness area of rugged grandeur, reminding seasoned

hikers of the Cederberg, with its bizarre rock formations. The imagination runs wild on the shapes formed by the weather-beaten rocks. But this area is far greener than the Cederberg, due to its higher rainfall. On top of which it's not nearly as hot. Surprisingly temperatures over 30 °C are rare, while down below in Porterville it's as hot as . . . No, don't say it.

Apart from the magnificent flora, the fauna is varied and plentiful, dominated perhaps by baboons – the only thieves you need worry about. The experts say it is easier to list the items not eaten by baboons than to try to count things they do eat. They are omnivorous and will steal your biltong out of your backpack as you sleep.

By way of a change return to Cape Town via Porterville, Gouda, Wellington, Agter Paarl and the N1. The distance is marginally shorter and the travelling time slightly longer, but the scenery is more attractive than the Malmesbury/Piketberg route.

To book call Cape Nature Conservation at Porterville (022) 931-2900.

Cape Times, March 17, 1995

Tree Tops

Dream about elephants
crashing through the forest below

Many people have heard of the famous Tree Tops Hotel in Kenya, where the young Princess Elizabeth learnt of her father's death and that she was to become queen.

One of the unique hotels in the world, it is visited by the wealthy and famous from all corners of the globe.

In contrast, few people know the secret of Citrusdal. All right, so it's not a full-on Tree Tops Hotel, but it is set in a poplar forest overhanging the Olifants River and has fully-equipped tree huts, all of which are interconnected by overhead walkways.

The huts are about 3,5 metres square, with balconies. They are equipped with bedding, crockery, cutlery, fridge and hotplate. A separate ablution block hangs in the trees. The huts and walkways are about four metres above the ground, so avoid sleepwalking. Especially under the ablution block.

This wonderful little gem of a getaway is a long way from anywhere, which adds to its charm. It is called Cardouw Country Retreat – the name is about to be changed to Tree Tops – and it lies 25 km

down a dead-end road running along the west bank of the Olifants River and past the well-known Warm Baths of Citrusdal.

Guests have a choice of two hiking trails. A short, ciruclar route around Salpeterkop takes about four hours. Part of this hike follows the route of the original Cardouw Pass over these mountains. This was used between about 1730 and 1850 and the grooves left by wagon wheels in the rocks can still be seen.

An early explorer and biologist, Carl Thunberg, described the pass as "the most difficult and precipitous road we have ever seen".

It's certainly not difficult to hike, but it does provide an insight into the hardships of the early settlers.

The alternative hike is an extension of the circular route and ends at the Warm Baths about eight hours later. What could be nicer than finishing a fairly strenuous hike with a soak in the healing waters?

The cost of this rustic hideaway-on-stilts is a modest R75 a night for each person – or R65 for weeknights. You will need to take your

own food and drinks, but all else is provided. Having a braaivleis on the balcony is definitely not a good idea, but plenty of place is provided on the neatly lawned banks of the Olifants River.

Tucked up in your bed in the trees, it's not difficult to imagine elephants crashing through the forest below you. Alas, they have long been gone.

To book, phone Niel or Milinda Bartie at (022) 921-3544 during office hours.

Sunday Times, July 21, 1996

Badkloof Trail

More than a pretty face
on Lover's Walk

Montagu is more than just a pretty face. It also has the ultimate in hikers' accommodation, as I discovered on a recent trip to once again do the Montagu Trail. The fact that we only did half the trail and gave the second day (Cogmanskloof) a miss speaks volumes for the quality of the accommodation we were privileged to be staying in.

The fact that it was around the 40 °C mark in the shade might have had something to do with our decision to abort, but not much. The prospect of lazing around a swimming pool in a delightful setting was just too tempting to ignore.

The Montagu Trail is a weekend hike that is really two one-day trails. Both start and end at the same point, the Klipspringer Hut. In this column on 2 December 1994 (see page 204), I wrote with great warmth about this hut (remember the schmaltz about the finest malt whisky in your hand and classical music bouncing off the surrounding cliffs)? Well, I've rediscovered heaven. Or at least something a lot more comfortable than the Klipspringer hut.

The town's grand old lady was starting to look her age. Having seen 120 summers, winter was starting to set in. So the Montagu Hotel was given a major facelift and renamed the Montagu Country Inn. The new name fits. And most important of all, it caters for hikers. What was originally the owner's house, built in 1905, has been turned into a hikers' cottage. They insist on calling it the Backpackers' facility, which tends to make it sound rather like a public convenience. However, it sleeps twenty people in five bedrooms with a TV lounge and self-catering kitchen. But the cherry on the top is the swimming pool.

All I could think of, coming down the gruelling descent of Bloupunt, was that sparkling swimming pool. Aren't we getting soft in our old age? A braai area, an open-air spa bath and typical platteland corner *kroeg* complete the picture.

And all this for the extremely modest sum of R28,50 per person per night. If you don't feel like a keen bean on the self-catering bit, then try the health breakfast of porridge (good carbo-loading stuff), fresh fruit (blood sugar booster) and

toast and coffee. All for R12,50.

In such relaxed surroundings, you could be excused for choosing a soft option when confronted by a formidable Montagu Trail in mid-summer with little water and no shade. Just such an option is there, in the 2,2-km Badkloof Trail along the so-called Lover's Walk from Ou Meul to the hot springs. It will only take thirty to forty minutes one way along a perfectly level path which winds its way along the floor of a deep and dramatic kloof. There is at least one good swimming hole along the way, enabling Badkloof to live up to its name.

At the Avalon Springs Hotel end of the kloof, there is a cave high above the valley floor, reached by means of some 250 steps built into the rock face. The view from the cave down onto Avalon Springs is captivating. The view into the cave is quite nauseating: graffiti "artists" have covered every square metre of this large cave with the products of their sick minds. Why on earth deface our beautiful mountains like this? Never have I seen such an appalling example of this public toilet mentality – not even in the backstreets of post-revolution Maputo.

Cool down on the return journey with a dip in the pool. You stand a pretty good chance of seeing klipspringer which seem to be quite unperturbed by your presence. Dassies and a pair of black eagles could just chase away your anger at the graffiti animals.

Montagu is certainly getting quainter and more gracious with age – unlike its ugly sister on the other side of the Cogmanskloof Pass, Ashton (pronounced Estin).

To book the Montagu Trail (no booking is needed for the Badkloof Trail) phone Mariette Barnes at the Montagu Municipality (0234) 42471. She will also be able to give you the numbers of a wide range of places to stay from hotels, lodges and guesthouses to self-catering farmhouses.

Cape Times, April 7, 1995

Lundy's top ten and farewell

Many magic paths

This column in one form or another has been bumbling along, on and off, for four-and-a-half years now. It's easy to say that it's time for a rest, or time to give my one-man business more attention (writing is my hobby, not my work), not to mention my extremely understanding and supportive wife. But the truth is, sooner or later you run out of walks.

And some 200 columns later, that's about the size of it. The only thing that surprises me is that there are so many hikes to write about in this wonderful corner of our country.

The mountains of the Cape hide so many magic places, hidden valleys, craggy peaks and cool streams. So it's difficult to name my favourites. They change with the weather and the seasons. But right now my top ten would be something like those listed below. In a few months time they may well have changed. But for now here are three far away (up to 1 000 km) from Cape Town, three nearby (up to 200 km) and four in the Peninsula.

The Otter Trail. The Prince of Trails cannot be left out of any-one's top ten. Unfortunately that's what everyone seems to think. Last year the National Parks Board received applications for accommodation for 68 000 people on the Otter Trail. There are only twelve places per day and 365 days in a year. Which means that it was over-subscribed by more than fifteen times. Put another way, you have about a seven per cent chance of being granted a permit. But don't give up hope. There are ways of increasing the odds. Work it out for yourself.

Amatola Trail in the Hogsback area of the Eastern Cape. If the Otter Trail is said to be the prince of trails, then the Amatola is surely king. It is said that if you do only one long trail in your life, then this should be the one.

But it's not a cakewalk at 105 km in six days. Everyone should have an emotional goal in life. If you're a hiker and you are fit, make this yours.

The Harkerville Trail between Knysna and Plettenberg Bay. This two-day trail through the Knysna forest and along the rugged coastline is a gem.

Arangieskop Trail near Robertson. My personal favourite, with two of the finest overnight huts in the Cape.

Die Hel in the Groot Winterhoek mountains above Porterville. If this is hell, I can't wait to get there.

Cederberg Wilderness Area. There is nothing like it anywhere else in the country. Memories of rock formations such as the Maltese Cross, Wolfberg Arch, Wolfberg Cracks, Stadsaal and Lot's Wife will stay with you for life.

Orange Kloof. After being closed to the public for the entire life of most Capetonians – more than sixty years – paradise has been reopened. Situated below Constantia Nek in the upper reaches of the Hout Bay valley, this is an arboreal *Jurassic Park*. Parts of it must be just as Van Riebeeck saw it when he described the area in his diary as having the finest forests in all of the world. Entry is very strictly by permit only and in the presence of a conservation officer. Call (021) 689-7438 (Newlands Forest) or (021) 713-0260 to book.

Chapman's Contour Path runs parallel to Chapman's Peak Drive at the base of the cliffs overlooking Hout Bay.

Suikerbossie Circuit starts and ends at the nek between Hout Bay and Llandudno. The route up Myburgh's Waterfall Ravine is very special, particularly in summer when hundreds of red disas put on a spectacular show.

Right Face-Arrow Face Traverse. This thrilling climb on the sheer face of Table Mountain is not for those with a fear of heights. No ropes needed, just nerves of steel. This is an exhilarating traverse along a narrow ledge which on two occasions seems to come to a dead end – only to continue *inside* the mountain, where the face of the mountain has literally shifted forward to leave a corridor behind, through which you can squeeze.

Au revoir and I hope to see you on the mountain.

Cape Times, July 31, 1998

Index

CAPE UNION MART STORES

CAPE TOWN Cnr Mostert & Corporation Str,
Tel (021) 464-5801; Fax: (021) 465-3566

CAPE TOWN WATERFRONT Shop 142, Victoria Wharf
Tel (021) 419-0019; Fax (021) 421-4480

CLAREMONT Shop 9 Cavendish Square
Tel (021) 674-2148; Fax (021) 674-1224

BLUE ROUTE Shop 51, Blue Route Centre, Retreat
Tel (021) 715-8470; Fax (021) 715-5991

N1 CITY Shop 93, N1 City Mall
Tel (021) 595-1220/1; Fax (021) 595-1478

TYGER VALLEY Shop 500 Tyger Valley Centre
Tel (021) 914-1441; Fax (021) 948-8702

SOMERSET WEST Shop 75, Somerset Mall
Tel (021) 852-7121; Fax (021) 851-6906

GARDENS Shop 54, Gardens Centre
Tel (021) 461-9678; Fax (021) 461-0686

GEORGE Shop B6, St George's Square Shopping Ctr
Tel (044) 871-4372/3; Fax (044) 871-4375

KNYSNA Shop 2, Woodmill Walk Shopping Ctr
Tel (044) 382-7588/9; Fax (044) 382-7590

HYDE PARK Shop LM66, Hyde Park Ctr
Tel (011) 325-5038; Fax (011) 325-5041

SANDTON CITY Shop U81A, Sandton City
  Tel (011) 884-9771; Fax (011) 884-9775

EASTGATE Shop U116, Eastgate Ctr
  Tel (011) 622-8779; Fax (011) 616-1135

FOURWAYS Shop G79, Fourways
  Tel (011) 465-9824/5/6; Fax (011) 465-9801

BROOKLYN Shop 201, Brooklyn Shopping Ctr, Pretoria
  Tel (012) 46-5511; Fax (012) 46-5667

NELSPRUIT Shop 71, Riverside Mall
  Tel (013) 757-0338; Fax (013) 757-0339

DURBAN Shop 306, 115 Musgrave Rd
  Tel (031) 210-231; Fax (031) 202-7081

PORT ELIZABETH Shop 60B, Walmer Park Shopping Ctr
  Tel (041) 368-7442/7413; Fax (041) 368-7413